Humanism
A Beginner's Guide

ONEWORLD BEGINNER'S GUIDES combine an original, inventive, and engaging approach with expert analysis on subjects ranging from art and history to religion and politics, and everything in-between. Innovative and affordable, books in the series are perfect for anyone curious about the way the world works and the big ideas of our time.

Beginners
GUIDES

Humanism
A Beginner's Guide

Peter Cave

ONEWORLD

A Oneworld Book

First published by Oneworld Publications in 2009
This updated edition first published in 2022

Copyright © Peter Cave 2009, 2022

ISBN 978-0-86154-356-4
eISBN 978-0-86154-357-1

Typeset by Geethik Technologies
Printed and bound in Great Britain by Clays Ltd, Elcograf S.p.A.

Oneworld Publications
10 Bloomsbury Street
London WC1B 3SR
England

MIX
Paper from
responsible sources
FSC® C018072

Contents

To the memory of
H. H. and G. V.
gentle man and gentle woman

Preface to the extended edition

May you live in interesting times.

Chinese curse (apocryphal)

Since the 2009 initial publication, a lot has happened. The happenings have not, of course, included proofs, to humanists' satisfaction, that God or gods exist – or proofs to religious believers' satisfaction that neither God nor gods exist. The many events have, though, continued to demonstrate the importance of humanist values: of respect for people; for freedom, fairness and fellow feeling – all without need of divine guidance.

The times, with worldwide disasters, have been interesting in the manner implied by the 'curse' epigraph; they should also have been painful for those humanists who believe adherence to humanist values makes it clear what ought to be done, whether the times be emergencies or more usual.

People, be they humanist or no, who see 'freedom' as the most glorious of values have had to live with pandemic lockdowns and borders closed to desperate migrants who flee oppressions or climate disorders by clinging onto flimsy boats in raging seas. My guess is that many lovers of freedom who oppose lockdowns and condemn restrictions to combat global warming are keen to keep border controls and keen to see them strengthened.

People, be they humanist or no, who value equality of respect have had to live with deeper inequalities in society – inequalities aggravated by the pandemic and responsive restrictions; by 'austerity', apparently essential in the wake of global financial crises; and, yes, by borders closed to desperate migrants in fearful flight.

My guess is that many lovers of equality, while vehemently arguing for more help for the disadvantaged, are reluctant to argue for open borders.

These two examples – freedom and equality of respect – remind us of how values conflict. Should freedom for the wealthy to buy their children superior education trump respect for poor families deserving of equal educational opportunities? Even with but one value in the frame, conflicts arise: is the freedom to drive noisy high-performance cars more important than people's freedom to enjoy undisturbed nights?

The book's first edition stressed how humanists – and others – need to recognize that values and applications cannot be easily measured one against another. We muddle through – as argued later. Religions provide no insulation from the muddles. 'God's word' still requires interpretation – whether within Judaism, Christianity, Islam or other faiths; even within one religion, fundamental disagreements persist over how lives ought to be lived.

Events since 2009 have included political crises, more natural disasters – wildfires, floods, droughts, earthquakes – together with war crimes, attempted genocides, terrorist attacks, revolutions and counter-revolutions. The rapid expansion of the internet, 'artificial intelligence' and big data collection has led to privacy intrusions and challenges to democracy, yet has enabled social media campaigns to increase awareness of certain discriminations (Black Lives Matter), sexual harassments (#MeToo) and dangers to planetary life (Extinction Rebellion). Those campaigns have, though, generated some chaos over free speech – with 'no-platforming' and arguments over who may say what to whom and where. There have also been some bizarre events.

In Paris in January 2015, two Islamic terrorists murdered staff of the satirical magazine *Charlie Hebdo*; its mockery of religion had included cartoons of the Prophet Mohammed. Over the next few days, further murders occurred, with police officers and a kosher supermarket attacked. That weekend, millions worldwide

– happily including 'Not In Our Name' Muslims – marched with the rallying cry *Je suis Charlie,* condemning the murders and defending democracy and free expression. Bizarrely, among the political leaders marching in Paris were those who maintained severe restrictions on free speech, restrictions which if broken could lead to floggings, imprisonment or death – leaders from, for example, Egypt, Turkey and the United Arab Emirates.

In 2017 Saudi Arabia was elected, by the usual secret ballot, for a four-year term to the United Nations Commission on the Status of Women, which promotes gender equality and women's empowerment. At the time, women in Saudi Arabia were still prohibited from driving; further, they needed a male guardian's permission to travel abroad. True, those particular restrictions have since been lifted, at least in law. Earlier, in 2013, Saudi Arabia was elected to the UN Human Rights Council, serving two consecutive three-year periods as permitted. Saudi Arabia, though, remains miles away from respecting human rights. Mind you, countries that trumpet human rights do not have impeccably clean hands. Julian Assange's 2010 WikiLeaks exposures of the United States' dubious diplomatic and military activities, some verging on war crimes, led not to governmental contrition, but to Assange's imprisonment, with his extradition and prosecution sought. Over the years, Britain has made plentiful arms sales to regimes that violently abuse human rights; weapons manufactured in the UK have, for example, been used by Saudi Arabia in the Yemeni Civil War, where bombings and blockades have led to a humanitarian catastrophe for Yemen's civilian population, with thousands dying and many more suffering.

On a smaller scale, there exist well-documented instances of Prime Minister Boris Johnson 'lying' in the House of Commons and declining to set the record straight. Bizarrely, members, when in the House, who declare the prime minister (or any MP) a liar are suspended. 'What does it matter, if politicians lie?' some may ask. Even if we ignore the intrinsic value of honesty, a humanist reply should be that it bodes badly for democracy when voters are misinformed and deliberately so.

Here are two more incongruity examples. Exceptionally well-paid female media presenters have rightly sought pay parity with male counterparts, yet both female and male presenters have curiously been coy in commenting on the vast pay discrepancies between presenters and workers such as nurses, care workers and cleaners. Protestors have marched demanding removal of statues of those whose vast wealth derived from slave-trading and other morally repugnant ways, yet they have rarely drawn attention to how their protesting, marching and reforming zeal rest on benefits from those ways. We are all entangled. The impossibility of making amends and redeeming ourselves without relying on past horrors needs, I suggest, express acknowledgement and humility.

Immanuel Kant, a major Enlightenment figure, a devotee of reason, respect and humanity, made an apt observation:

> Out of the crooked timber of humanity no straight thing was ever made.

Humanists seek to do their best in straightening things out. The preceding examples show how there are bound to be conflicts, incongruities and inconsistencies – and how crookedness will persist.

Two significant global dangers reviewed in this extended edition are pandemics and climate change. Chapter 8 discusses some conflicted and crooked thinking in handling them, while Chapter 9 takes matters further into the realm of ever-expanding cyberspace, human enhancements, posthumanism – and 'the end'.

When two philosophers meet, recommended Ludwig Wittgenstein, they should say, 'Take your time.' When humanists meet and disagree – all the more so, when humanists meet and agree – they should take their time and reflect. Rarely are there easy answers. To readers dipping into this book, I recommend: take your time.

Prologue

Let us be human.

I began writing this book on a Christmas Eve, listening to A Festival of Nine Lessons and Carols, broadcast from King's College Chapel, Cambridge, yet I am a humanist, an atheistic humanist. Atheistic humanism does not have to reject the sacred and uplifting – and it need not deny that such life enhancements are often found in religion. True, humanism typically rejects religions; yet it is, using words of John Stuart Mill, 'enemy of no religions but those that appear injurious either to reasoning powers or moral sentiments'. Of course, that includes a lot.

As I finished this book, I happened to be in radio dialogue with a kindly, though radically misinformed Father of the Catholic Church – misinformed, that is, about humanism. He stressed Christian values, values that he opposed to humanism's 'utility'. When asked what he meant, he said that humanists lacked objective values, having mere subjective ones to do with usefulness. This book, I hope, will help to dispel such mistaken beliefs. It is no essential part of humanism to reject objective values – far from it. Humanism values human dignity. Yes, some humanist philosophers speak of utility; but utility is understood as happiness or promotion of happiness, happiness involving faring well, through valuing friendships, honesty, compassion, and much of the world around us.

This book is, of course, for readers interested in humanism, its underlying philosophy, and criticisms of its position. Hence it also provides an introduction for readers interested in ethics, political philosophy and the philosophy of religion, with arguments concerning God's existence, morality, the place of religion in politics, and the possibility of godless yet meaningful lives. As this book forms part of an introductory series, I have not cluttered the main text with notes, sources and references. Clutter duly occurs, with further readings, at the end.

I hope that the work will possess wide appeal: to religious believers as well as to unbelievers – to those certain of their stance, be it as believer or no, and to those uncertain. The chapter titles are self-explanatory, though I should comment that a medley of important themes, themes not usually emphasized, is played within Chapter 7 and the Epilogue (despite the danger that some, unable to believe in humanist sincerity, may regard references to religious music and poetry as self-serving) and in Chapters 8 and 9 where even extinction comes to the fore. This book is not, by the way, dealing with humanistic psychology, which stands opposed to behaviourism. It looks at humanism as broadly understood: a humanism concerned with a godless understanding of the world and values.

My formal philosophical education began at University College London, as a godless student of Gower Street. The college was formed, with the support of Jeremy Bentham and the Mills (father and son, James and John Stuart Mill), in the early nineteenth century. It was the first British university that lacked Church of England religious tests, permitting entrance by atheists, agnostics, humanists, the religious and all – well, given the times, for the first few decades the all were male. At the college today, in the Department of Philosophy, there lacks the encouragement to agree – and humanists are happy *not* to agree. Humanism is a broad church. So, although in recent years, I have chaired the Humanist Philosophers' Group – and much of this book's content is typical of humanist thinking – my words express no official doctrine; they are slave to no party line and are sometimes critical of some common humanist thought. Happily, we are here not engaged in analyses of arcane disputes within and between official humanist, atheist, rationalist and secularist organizations.

Some people seek sharp definitions of terms – for all the necessary and sufficient conditions – but that is often a mistake, a mistake exposed by Ludwig Wittgenstein. Many terms are 'family resemblance' terms, where there are criss-crossing resemblances and differences between items on the basis of which the terms apply. Humanists, in their humanism, possess a variety of beliefs about the nature of morality, the good life, how best to understand the relationship between mind and body, and so on. In an introductory work of this size, it would be impossible to cover all approaches that have been labelled 'humanist'; it would also be undesirable. What follows sometimes has my own humanist predilections and idiosyncrasies on display, while setting out the approaches, beliefs – ethos – of many of today's humanists.

Some religious believers see humanists, atheists and agnostics as devils spreading intellectual corruption and evil ways. Such believers burn books. Well, to use an observation of Steve Jones the geneticist and humanist: I do not mind if the religious burn my books, so long as they buy them first.

A few years ago my father, then my mother, died. They both were Christians. When things were particularly bad, their faith undoubtedly brought them some comfort. During those final years, it would have been unkind, unhelpful – and in bad taste – for me to have challenged their beliefs. They were sensitive people; and that I possess at least some sensitivity I owe to them and give thanks to them – to H. H. and G. V.

The death of parents – of relatives, friends and colleagues, believers or not – causes most of us to become more reflective, sensing our humanity, fragilities and inevitable losses. Such awareness should encourage some of my more robust humanist colleagues to resist attacking the religious at every opportunity. There are times and places; there are seasons. So, while I hope that many religious believers will read this book and lose their belief, often a dangerous belief, I also hope that this book will remain unopened by kindly people in desperate circumstances, people who would feel even more desperate if their faith were undermined at this moment. I trust, though, that many religious believers will come to see that belief in God is not required for morality, for comprehending the world and for leading fulfilling lives for selves and others.

'Let us be human' captures our humanist theme, directing eyes to ourselves, living here in the world – though the injunction has been used by diverse philosophers, both believers and unbelievers, from Spinoza to Hume, from Kierkegaard to Wittgenstein. It is even quoted by Polly the parrot in the Hans Christian Andersen tale *The Magic Galoshes*. 'Let us be human' therefore needs sensitive handling: if we are not careful, it may set us spinning away from reality. As A. E. Housman irreverently writes, 'And malt does more than Milton can/To justify God's ways to man.'

It is true that, in the following pages, I cannot resist the odd quip at religion's expense, but I, and other humanists, intend no harm to anyone who values much about humanity and the world in general. Religious believers who read this book may come to realize that humanists are – well – humans, humans who emphasize the good in humanity, while not ignoring humanity's many frailties, disagreeable features and worse. Indeed, the more that people reflect on the humanist stance the nearer they may come to realizing that they too are humanists, with no need for belief in God.

1
Humanism: scene setting

> Only connect! That was the whole of her sermon. Only connect
> the prose and the passion, and both will be exalted, and human
> love will be seen at its height. Live in fragments no longer. Only
> connect, and the beast and the monk, robbed of the isolation
> that is life to either, will die.
>
> E. M. Forster

Understanding the world without God, giving sense to the world without God, is the heart of today's humanism. There are two segments here: understanding how things are; understanding how things ought to be. This is the distinction between facts and values, though arguably there is no sharp boundary. In each segment the humanistic stance is that we can, and should, flourish – one way or another – without God. Humanists speak of humanism making sense of the world using reason, experience and shared human values. Humanists encourage us to make the best of our lives, lives containing meaning and purpose, without resort to superstitions and the supernatural. That people are concerned for others, can empathize, feel and imagine as well as reason, test and evaluate, simply is true; and, when we feel alienated from others, it is worth calling to mind the twentieth-century novelist and humanist E. M. Forster and his 'Only connect!'

We have spoken starkly. Here is a caveat. Some religious believers, Jews, Christians, Muslims and others speak of themselves as humanists and they engage in humanitarian activities. According to mainstream humanists though, belief in Yahweh, God or Allah, if the belief is suitably tepid or humanized, at best adds nothing of value to godless humanism; at worse, if the belief is stringent and literal, it is highly dangerous to both reason and morality. Religion, here, is understood as essentially involving belief in God or gods, where the belief generates doctrines of morality and how life should be lived, involving attention to scriptures, rituals and salvation. For ease, we shall usually drop the qualifier of 'or gods'; we assume that humanist arguments against God's existence can be suitably modified to apply to gods of polytheistic religions.

Unless implied otherwise, we take it that when people talk of God, they are talking of a supreme immaterial being, all powerful, all good and all knowing, standing in some continuing personal relationship with humans. Deists are more austere, believing God to be little more than the creator-designer. For further ease, we shall often refer to religious believers, be they Jew, Christian or Muslim, or some other variety, as 'theists', the context making it clear which believing features are relevant. God, traditionally understood as a really existent being, holding a personal relationship with human beings, is what God is for millions and millions of Jews, Christians and Muslims – whatever some academic theologians may say. True, some thinkers, such as the nineteenth-century Ludwig Feuerbach, see theology as anthropology, arguing that God is, in some way, humanity's projection of human ideals; but that is not the understanding of most religious believers. True, some believing theologians do see God in a light radically different from that of an existent being: in Chapter 3, we blink, a little, in that light – and we blink sympathetically. Humanists have no good reason to reject, for example, belief in God if all that amounts to is the encouragement to love thy neighbour – well, I suppose it can depend on the neighbours.

This book is about current mainstream humanism, humanism that lacks godly belief, where 'godly belief' is taken as the traditional belief in God. It is a humanism which does not collapse into relativism; hence, there is but the occasional passing wave at relativists and those of a postmodernist persuasion. 'Humanism' throughout is the current mainstream, unless context implies otherwise – and the context is otherwise, later in this chapter, when we briefly look at 'humanism' in history. Chapters thereafter run through some key humanist stances of today together with criticisms of those stances.

The greatest weight

Let us approach these matters further by means of a rather bizarre thought, a thought from the nineteenth-century philosopher Friedrich Nietzsche. In rejecting religion, Nietzsche is at one with today's humanism; but his rejection of much traditional morality and his questioning of truth places him at odds with typical humanists. Here is Nietzsche's greatest weight:

> What if, some day or night, a demon were to steal into your loneliest loneliness and say to you:
>
> This life as you now live it and have lived it, you will have to live once again and innumerable times again; and there will be nothing new in it, but every pain and every joy and every thought and sigh and everything unspeakably small or great in your life must return to you, all in the same succession and sequence – even this spider and this moonlight between the trees, and even this moment and I myself. The eternal hourglass of existence is turned over again and again, and you with it, speck of dust!
>
> Would you not throw yourself down and gnash your teeth and curse the demon who spoke thus? ... Or how well disposed

would you have to become to yourself and to life – *to long for nothing more fervently* than this ultimate eternal confirmation and seal?

This greatest weight is nonsensical, leading to absurdity (to be seen in Chapter 7); yet it may impel us to ask: how ought we to live?

How ought we to live? Humanism tritely answers: with truth, not illusion; with morality, not immorality; with tolerance, not repression. In contrast, according to humanists, religions are grounded in illusion, threaten morality, and often show little tolerance. Of course, the religious see matters in reverse. Humanists, though, point to the irrational groundings of religions. Through scriptures, revelations and alleged miracles – through bishops, rabbis and imams – religions aim to permeate believers' lives, their daily toils, sexual behaviour, even permitted music. Humanism lacks scriptures, revelations and miracles; it lacks bishops, rabbis and imams. Humanists do not burn books, threaten eternal damnation, or take offence at anti-humanist cartoons.

Humanists rely on our common humanity. Some critics, atheist even, regard this as making humanity into God, a god to be worshipped here on earth; but contemporary humanism typically is committed to nothing of the kind. Humanism simply recognizes that human beings have similar basic needs, interests and values; and, through our rationality and fellow feeling, we can lead good, cooperative and meaningful lives. Life does not become empty and meaningless in a godless universe. Apart from this outlook outlined, humanists do not conform to any stereotype. Today's humanists range from those happy to tend their family and garden, to those who seek artistic success alone, to those who fight for political reform, be it on the political right or political left – to those who save the whale.

What is the relationship between humanism, atheism and agnosticism? In today's terminology, atheists believe there are no

HUMANIST VOICES

It is said that the Devil has all the best tunes. Whether or not true, humanist lyrics often go unnoticed. Maybe that is because they are sensible, reasonable and usually sung somewhat quietly, not ranted from mountaintops, preached from pulpits. Many distinguished voices are humanist even though with no 'humanist' label. Humanist voices, with or without the label, deserve to be heard – such as:

Charles Darwin: I cannot persuade myself that a beneficent and omnipotent God would have designedly created parasitic wasps with the express intention of their feeding within the living bodies of Caterpillars.

Ralph Waldo Emerson: You take the way from man, not to man.

Mark Twain: God's inhumanity to man makes countless thousands mourn.

Albert Einstein: A man's ethical behaviour should be based effectually on sympathy, education, and social ties; no religious basis is necessary. Man would indeed be in a poor way if he had to be restrained by fear of punishment and hope of reward after death.

Richard Rorty: The utopian social hope which sprang up in nineteenth-century Europe is still the noblest imaginative creation of which we have record.

Philip Pullman: The true end of human life … is not redemption by a non-existent Son of God, but the gaining and transmission of wisdom.

We could add today, for example, the voices of Salman Rushdie and Jonathan Miller, Terry Pratchett and Christopher Hitchens, Margaret Atwood and Richard Dawkins. From earlier times, we would hear Thomas Hardy, James Joyce, Bernard Shaw and Manabendra Nath Roy. Earlier, we find David Hume, Benjamin Franklin, John Stuart Mill and Giuseppe Verdi – to mention a few.

gods; agnostics leave things open, suspending belief. Today's humanism is, then, 'atheism–agnosticism plus', the plus being the belief in shared human values and rationality.

From Midwest America's Christian fundamentalisms to Middle Eastern and Far Eastern Muslims, many believers understand that their duty is to convert, or deal in some way with, non-believers – with 'devils in disguise'. This affects their ethics, politics and daily living, leading some determined to bring non-believers to see the religious light or, at least, to live according to religious law. When humanists become vocal about the dangers of religion, they therefore are not making a big fuss about kindly and tolerant Church of England vicars who share tea and cucumber sandwiches with parishioners. They are rightly making a big fuss about those whose godly belief leads to the repression of many here on earth, be it through death threats to questioners of religious belief, or punishment to women who dare to remove the veil in public.

We are all 'atheists'

Our use of 'atheism' carries no moral disapproval or threat of burning at the stake, though historically such has often been dished out to those so deemed – and dished out in the name of 'caring' religion. Fortunately, dealing with atheists in this manner in the West is largely out of vogue. It is indeed fortunate, if we, for literary effect, in the next paragraph, weaken our understanding of 'atheist' to the denial of some gods or other.

We are all atheists – to varying extents. The 'we' includes Jews, Christians, Muslims and other godly believers. We reject the existence of – well, allow me to mention but a few, from a spectacular rolling display that has involved a cast of thousands, from the nasty to nice. There are the Olympian gods: Aphrodite, Apollo, Ares, Artemis, Athene, Demeter, Dionysus, Hades,

Hephaistos, Hera, Hermes, Hestia, Persephone, Poseidon and Zeus – and many more. Here are some African gods: Abassi, Anansi, Babalu-aye, Bumba, Elegua, Eshu, Obatala, Olorun, Shango and Yemaya. Now for some Nordic gods: Baldur, Freya, Frigg, Idun, Loki, Odin, Thor and Tyr. We could pop along to many other parts of the world, listing yet more and more. Let us not pretend all such colourful gods have vanished from people's beliefs, with the religious all believing in one transcendent being. Some still worship the gods of Olympus; druid ceremonies involve pagan worship. Millions of Hindus worship a baffling array of gods, for example, the Vedic and Vaishnava gods – though maybe they are but facets of Brahman. Christians and Muslims are committed to the one God – the same one God? – yet they often assert the existence of other supernatural beings, namely angels and the Devil.

That millions have believed and do believe in gods and other supernatural powers should not, of course, lead us to conclude that there are such gods and powers, not least because many of the believed gods and powers rule out the others. It is worth making that obvious point because sometimes believers in solely one god, namely, God, shore up belief by observing that so many people are religious believers.

Humanism's rejection of God leads some to insist that humanism is negative. That is no more a legitimate accusation than that religion is negative, being a rejecter of the natural as all there is. True, the term 'atheist' is etymologically grounded in 'not' and 'god'. The use of the term 'atheist' is a tribute to religion's power: the presumption has been in favour of theism. After all, we do not believe in fairies, witches and scientific entities such as phlogiston, yet lack terms such as a-fairyist, a-witchist or a-phlogistonist. To avoid the theistic playing ground, suggestive of their being only 'anti' something, many humanists avoid 'atheist' and opt, for example, for 'rationalist' or 'naturalist', each of which points away from the supernatural.

Curiously, a staunch and outspoken humanist, namely, Richard Dawkins, who often promotes himself as strongly atheistic, takes the line that you cannot prove a negative. Hence, he reluctantly concludes that it is hugely unlikely that God exists, but, none the less, he is not absolutely certain. Indeed, I recall a radio interview when Dawkins was challenged as being committed to certainties, his reply being, 'Certainly not!'

The reluctance to be certain of God's non-existence may result from confusion. What counts as a negative? Is 'bald' negative, referring to no hair; or is 'hairy' negative, referring to no baldness? Either way, we can be certain that some people are bald and some not. I can prove that there are neither elephants nor round squares in this room. It may be thought more difficult to prove a negative, when it involves denying an item's existence *anywhere* in the universe. Modifying a much used example from Bertrand Russell, can we disprove the existence of a teapot somewhere beyond our solar system? Well, it seems odd to insist that we should be a little uncertain. We have not the faintest reason or evidence to believe in such a teapot. Furthermore, concerning God, he is not like a teapot. God is not typically thought of, these days, as an object to be found somewhere in space; so, it is not even clear what is involved in finding him. The search for God is no hunting expedition.

A general point is this. If you are justified in being certain that something is so, it does not follow that it is so. You are, no doubt, certain that no one popped a diamond in your pocket this week without your noticing, but removed it a few minutes later, also without your noticing. Yet, of course, it is possible that you are mistaken. Does that mean that you should be a little bit agnostic about the matter? Obviously not.

Whether humanists prefer to think of themselves as atheists or agnostics, they look only to the actual world around them including human beings, rather than to supernatural agents. The

Humanists ask religious believers:

To those who ground morality in God: were there no God, would deceiving, torturing and killing be acceptable?
To the religiously faithful: what is your response to those who base terrorism and oppression on faith?
To those who say that, without God, the universe is a mystery: is not God a mystery?
To those who believe in immortal souls: how can immortal souls be what persons really are?
To those with god-inspired meaningful lives: what is the meaning for billions suffering now on earth and eternally in hell?

Religious believers ask humanists:

Whatever can justify moral principles, if there is no God?
Is not humanism also a religion, a leap of faith, in humanity?
Why is the world life-giving, comprehensible and beautiful?
Without a soul, is not a person just a lump of matter?
How can lives have meaning, if death is utter annihilation?

natural–supernatural distinction, though, is not easy to identify: some theists speak of seeing God 'in' nature. Our use, here, of 'natural' points just to those concepts which both believers *and* non-believers alike use when talking about the world – about tables and chairs, people cycling and falling in love, molecular structures and photons. References to angels or the Devil or God, if meant literally, are supernaturalistic. Of course, we still have problems: who knows which concepts physicists will be employing next century? What we can truthfully say is that humanism does not make use of beings that go beyond our common experience, scientific evidence and reasoning, in order to understand the world. And perhaps that is the best we can say.

We are all human valuers

We all value some things – but that alone does not mean that we all value the same things. Humanists speak of holding human values, but what are those values? If they are whatever it is that humans value, well, of course, millions and millions value their relationship, as they see it, to God – a value on the humanist reject list. Some people place their own immediate self-interest as of highest value; that value rating is not usually humanism's. Humanism's values are grounded in features of human flourishing.

Many theists view humanists as devoid of spirituality and morality: humanists are crude materialists, ignorant of life's finer immaterial aspects. True, many humanists are materialists, but they are not thereby money grabbing, living only for consumer goods. Materialism, in this context, is simply the theory that the universe, including thoughts and feelings, can in some way be understood as material. With the discoveries of electrons, protons and much more, the term 'matter' has more or less disappeared from science: materialism is better spoken of as 'physicalism'. Physicalism does not deny the existence of rainbows, the feelings of awe at sunsets and the intoxications of love. Just because these items – the spiritual – can be explained in scientific terms (if they can), they are not thereby unreal.

Look around us, say many theists, and we see the effects of being blind to God. Scan secular societies: there are broken homes, sexual abuse, lives ruined through drugs, and increases in crime. Some theists, even today in the West, identify the increased ravages of nature – through tsunamis and hurricanes – as resulting from spiritual decline. 'Humanists are, indeed, devils in disguise, if any disguise there be.' Of course, humanists rebut this outrageous slur. Loss of religion does not have to generate the unhappy results cited – and usually does not. Furthermore, religions have caused much that merits challenge – the torturing and killing of people out of kilter with the preferred religious beliefs. Humanists, though, are not blind to the fact that religious believers are *humans*. In promoting shared human values, humanists do not, of course, promote whatever it is about humans that lead them to commit atrocious acts. Also, humanists are not ignorant of the horrors performed without a religious basis – be they of the Holocaust, of the numerous wars around the globe, from Vietnam, Cambodia and Laos years ago, to the more recent atrocities in Rwanda, Darfur and Zimbabwe, to the various continuing repressions in China, Myanmar, Afghanistan and elsewhere. Humanists know very, very well that humans can be incredibly nasty. Such nastiness is one reason why humanists encourage humanism – to promote the good features of humanity.

Humanists and theists sometimes play counting games. Have humanists produced more good – or more harm – than Jews, Christians or Muslims? This is futile number swapping. First, humanists and theists disagree over harms: converting from Islam to Christianity, women in public unveiled – are these harms? Secondly, actions performed may lack accord with the correct understanding of humanism or the religion. Were Christians who supported slavery rightly following the Bible? Are the imams who aim to destroy Jews reading the Qur'an correctly? Thirdly, a whole range of background beliefs may also be relevant behavioural factors. Fourthly, competing values may help to secure improvements; perhaps the best games are those with some would-be cheaters, keeping others on guard. What can be said by humanists – and rightly so – is that some religious doctrines, as opposed to humanistic ones, explicitly encourage harmful actions against non-believers just because they are non-believers. Humanism promotes societies that tolerate religions; many religious believers are not remotely keen on societies that tolerate free-thinking humanists.

Science, soul, and a fading God

Sciences or humanities? Today, in schools, universities and personality testing, there is a rough and ready distinction between those inclined towards the humanities – the arts, languages, literature, feeling – and those inclined towards the sciences, the analytic, reason and structured experiments. Mathematics is usually placed in the latter category; philosophy in the former – both subjects alerting us to the falsity of sharp boundaries. Whatever the distinction's strength – in the mid-twentieth century, C. P. Snow spoke sadly of 'two cultures' – 'humanism' of the past aided the development of both arenas; and today's humanism maintains a presence in both, valuing both science and the humanities. Here follows a brief series of snapshots of the term 'humanism', related terms and their changing use.

Ancient Rome's 'humanitas' focused on education in the values revealed through language and literature, history and moral philosophy. A term near to our 'humanism', namely *'umanista*, entered the fifteenth-century academic jargon in Renaissance Italy, for teachers and students of the humanitas, particularly through the writings of the Roman orator Cicero. As understanding of classical Greek developed, the ancient Greek philosophers were added to the canon. England, late on the scene, produced 'humanist' a century later – and 'humanism', in noun form, first appeared in Germany, very early in the nineteenth century.

Renaissance humanists, although typically Christian, were fascinated by pre-Christian cultures, their studies tending to be humanity- rather than God-centred. Overall, 'humanism' marked a commitment to classical literature and the humane values within. 'Humanism' is still used today within academic circles for that scholarly interest. Studying the classics led Renaissance humanists to be more open-minded than many of their medieval predecessors; they were also often more modest, aware of limitations on our understanding of God. Aristotle had, indeed, wisely written that one should not aim at certainty beyond the nature of the case.

Renaissance humanism focused on humanity's perceived uniqueness; important humanists Erasmus and Rabelais highlighted, for example, humour. Talk of 'the dignity of man' was prominent, with humanity glorified by Petrarch, Marsilio Ficino, Pico and Pietro Pomponazzi. Petrarch climbed Mont Ventoux, awed by the magnificent view, but then became angry at his admiring earthly things, overlooking humanity's wonders. Ficino saw humans, in his astronomical understanding, as somewhat god-like. Pomponazzi judged that being a human for one year was more perfect than an oak tree for ten thousand. Although the Bible spoke of humanity's fall, Renaissance thinkers laid greater emphasis on humans being made in God's image, superior to non-human animals.

The dignity of humanity is closely associated with Pico's 1486 oration (though the title, 'On the Dignity of Man', was added later and not by Pico). Pico described human beings as of no fixed nature, in contrast to non-human animals, humans possessing the freedom to choose how to be. This theme was taken up, centuries later, with the existentialist anguish over choosing our values, most famously presented by Jean-Paul Sartre in 1930/40s Paris.

Not all humanists trumpeted humanity's dignity. In early sixteenth-century Florence, Niccolò Machiavelli, while arguing for the glory of leaders, spoke of humankind's grabbing, deceitful and corrupt nature. Machiavelli, apparently encouraging political leaders to use religion for their own ends, became the arch atheist, whence the term 'old Nick'. In sixteenth-century France, Michel de Montaigne focused on humanity's weaknesses, foibles and modest place in the universe. In Britain, Francis Bacon, arguably, followed a similar line. Although Montaigne was a practising Catholic and Bacon attended Anglican services, in their writings and conduct they made little use of God and the quest for eternal salvation.

Earlier, medieval historians had often read natural events as divine rewards or punishments, but the humanist approach, developing scientific exploration, gave diminishing space to the divine. Humans were responsible for society's happenings; and laws of nature explained what happened in the surrounding natural world. Such naturalistic explanations, explanations in terms of physical events causing other physical events, contrasted with, say, Samuel Pepys's seventeenth-century belief. Pepys spoke of colds as divine retribution for illicit flirtations. In the next century, lightning more than once shattered St Mark's bell tower in Venice. Benjamin Franklin recommended conducting rods. St Mark's clergy opposed such new-fangled solutions: one ought not to meddle with providence by controlling God's artillery. Wiser counsel eventually won through, anticipating Lichtenberg who erected a lightning rod in 1780, noting that sermons are no substitute for such rods.

Major figures who sought to understand the world's mechanism – Descartes and Newton in the seventeenth century – were still awed by Christianity. Descartes used God to justify reliance on human reason and the senses. Newton thought of space as constituted by God's omnipresence. Later, though, experimentation and reasoning made little reference to divine purposes. We find the great eighteenth-century philosophers, David Hume and Immanuel Kant, both putting God in his place, a place with nothing to do – and, for Hume, not even the doing of existing. Today's humanists tend to applaud the good-humoured Hume and his witty attacks on religion and superstition. Kant, awoken from his 'dogmatic slumbers' by reading Hume, promoted the motto 'Sapere aude' – dare to know; have the courage of your reason. He wrote of the Enlightenment as the time when many thinkers placed reason, individual conscience and self-legislation above dictates of church and state. Today's humanist thinkers do likewise. Kant was committed to humanity's autonomy, the power of reason and the search for truth. Today's humanists tend to have similar commitments, yet lack Kant's confidence.

Reflection and reason led Kant to ever-increasing admiration of the starry heavens above and moral law within, neither beyond humanity's comprehension. Reflection and experimentation led others to see humans as machines. La Mettrie wrote his radically materialist *L'Homme Machine* in 1747, so radical and dangerous that other Enlightenment *philosophes*, for example, Voltaire and Diderot, took a step away. In its extreme, this is scientism. Scientism asserts that there can be a unified scientific understanding of every aspect of the world, including human beings. Descriptions of human activities and values can be reduced to talk about molecules, genes, neural circuits or whatever is within the scientists' vocabulary. The objectivity and superiority of such understanding is to be established by its predictive powers. In the early nineteenth century, we find Auguste Comte developing sociology, with biology, as a means of predicting human behaviour and aiding social reform. Various other social reformers – Jeremy Bentham and Robert Owen spring to mind, and, much later, B. F. Skinner – sought to understand human behaviour and society in order to control people, albeit with the overarching aim of humankind's overall benefit, often without Christian reliance on immortal souls.

Humanism need not buy into scientism; and, certainly, mainstream humanists argue that humans should be free to make their own decisions about how to live, without behavioural manipulation. Humanists, though, often give a friendly wave vaguely in support of everything being grounded in the physical. In contrast, some of us – and I write as an atheistic humanist – believe that whatever the scientific progress, there will remain features resistant to that type of understanding, features of human life that depend on interpretation, meaning and the individual's viewpoint. This is not to re-introduce the supernatural with souls, immortality or God. It is the happy acceptance of there being more to understanding than scientific understanding. Whatever causal explanations of hand movements through neurological changes, arguably they would not explain the movements' significance – whether the person was doodling, practising signatures or drawing – and would not be giving the person's reasons, such as 'I promised to write the cheque'. Education in the humanities, in the appreciation of poetry, music, sunsets and, indeed, other people, is recognition of this. This recognition runs the danger, when in the wrong hands, of dismissing scientific understanding completely, ignoring the huge beneficial significance of scientific successes in all our lives. It also runs the danger of being assimilated to seemingly bizarre postmodernist claims about 'all is interpretation' and 'there are no facts', claims that, at least on the surface, are as silly as they are self-refuting. Such claims do not belong to today's mainstream humanism.

Enlightenment values of reason and autonomy continue to hold sway for many humanists. Many, though, are sceptical of any metaphysical suggestion that reason and rationality constitute humanity's essence. Many would reject the concept of 'essence' applied here. Indeed, in the nineteenth and early twentieth centuries, the American pragmatists, from Ralph Waldo Emerson and Charles Peirce to William James and John Dewey, emphasized humanity, human dignity and the importance of scientific investigation, yet did question quite what constituted truth and reason – and certainly sought no fixed essence of humankind. Such pragmatic humanists may be seen as meliorists, hopeful of human progress, yet without viewing human beings as standing separate from environmental impingings. This tradition more recently found voice through Richard Rorty, reason itself also coming under something of an attack.

In Europe, Sartre, with his existentialist humanism, rejected a fixed human nature, but gave confident pride of place to autonomy. Sartre rejected God; but earlier, Peirce became tied to a pantheism and James valued mystical experiences. To add to the melee, we have Marxist humanism, where, contrary to the above, there is talk of species essence. We also have the linguistic obscurities of Martin Heidegger's 1947 *Letter on Humanism*. Hence, happy is my prefatorial comment that this book is staying within current mainstream humanism.

According to one influential recent writer – John Gray – humanists deny that humans are part of the animal kingdom, insist that only human interests are important, and believe humans are masters of their destiny, committed to progress. Such claims are woolly and need clarification, but, as they stand, they misunderstand today's humanism. Gray seems unaware that humanists read their Darwin, save the whale and that some of us are pretty pessimistic, only too well aware of humanity's flaws. Humanists, Gray adds, believe that by knowing the truth, humans are free. Try telling that to prisoners who know the truth, namely, that they are in chains.

Of course, some humanists have been, and are, optimistic about improving the lot of humankind. Some have used the phrase 'religion of humanity' – including Comte and then John Stuart Mill, though in very different senses. Comte, for example, no supporter of democracy, proposed a secular sociological priesthood to provide society with spiritual and moral guidance. In the early twentieth-century American literary world, we find the New Humanists who, arguing in the opposite direction, believed that human beings were unique, their wills in some way free of deterministic laws. Manabendra Nath Roy's New Humanism in India promoted human rationality as the universe expressing itself, with a continuous expansion of human freedom through greater and greater knowledge.

A formal sharp-edged definition of 'humanism', embracing all these features, is then impossible. What we can say is that, without commitment to a particular metaphysics, the humanist stance today typically values empirical investigation and reason; recognizes that people can, at least on the surface, make choices about how to live their lives; insists that they should be allowed to do so, when not harming others; and places a high value on concern for others. That, in contrast, 'humanism' has been used by some to describe their state authoritarianism, their religion or commitment to a theory of humankind's essence, no more means that today's mainstream humanism is committed to such than that religious believers burned heretics during the Inquisition means that today's Quakers are committed to burning non-believers. Humanism of today needs be committed neither to the existence of a fixed human nature, nor to a faith in humanity as essentially separate from nature, nor to a social utopia.

As today's humanists are usually atheists, or at least agnostics, a few words on the history of atheism are in order.

In contrast to 'humanism', historically the term 'atheism' was abusive, indicative of immorality and lawlessness. It was not applied, in today's sense, as merely to those who lacked belief in God. The 'atheist' label was often attached to people who were Christians, but guilty of heresy. Much of Europe was, of course, dominated by churches and the Church. The pre-Christian ancient Greeks and Romans had been surrounded by temples; yet, those days, before a powerful monotheistic religion took hold, saw thinkers blatantly declaring their atheism often without significant danger. Protagoras, a Greek sophist of the fifth century BCE, was deemed atheist, yet maintained a good reputation. He was unable to discover whether the gods existed and what they would be like: the matter, he said, was obscure; and life was short. We also meet the atomists – Leucippus, Democritus and Epicurus – who had no place for gods, the world being understood as an array of moving atoms.

In centuries much closer to home, in continental Europe, atheism, as now understood, was emerging. It was defended in Baron d'Holbach's eighteenth-century *The System of Nature*, which propounded a radical materialism. It received a public burning; the Baron did not – he had wisely arranged anonymous publication. Father Meslier wrote, earlier, secretly and voluminously on how he came to see that God did not exist. The work was published, after his death in 1733, by Voltaire, courtesy of Swiss safety. In America, Thomas Paine and Thomas Jefferson were casting doubts on God and religion. By the nineteenth century in Britain, we have George Holyoake speaking of 'secularism'; and a brave soul, so to speak, was Charles Bradlaugh who explicitly proclaimed himself atheist. When elected Northampton's Member of Parliament and seeking to enter the House of Commons, he was prepared to swear oaths on the Bible, prepared because, lacking belief, such swearing was irrelevant. The authorities failed to see it in such a kindly, sensible way. He reaped temporary imprisonment and dismissal.

Atheistic thinkers, by the early twentieth century – Bertrand Russell, John Maynard Keynes, Jean-Paul Sartre – could express their atheism without endangering life, but, in Russell's case, sometimes endangering livelihood. Many politicians today are atheistic humanists, yet who, certainly in America, keep quiet, fearful of losing votes. More seriously, as you read these words, some, even in Western Europe, are hounded because of speaking freely on religion: witness the death threats some Muslims directed at the humanist writer Salman Rushdie; recall the murder of Theo van Gogh because of his film about abuse of Muslim women. And, more widely, throughout the world, thousands of people are indiscriminately maimed or killed because they lack the right religious belief, wear the wrong clothing, or are in the wrong place.

* * *

In view of the importance of godly belief in many lives, we shall – in Chapter 2 – examine key arguments for the existence of God and the humanist atheistic response. Of course, however good the arguments are for a divine creator-designer, they fail to show that such a being is Yahweh who chose the Jews; or is in some way identical with Jesus Christ, a man sent down on earth to be killed and resurrected; or is identical with Allah of Islam. Proving a creator-designer's existence, without knowing anything else about the being, is of no direct relevance to how we live and should live our lives; hence, many theists turn to personal revelation and scripture. Millions, though – at all levels and despite what some re-interpreters of religion say – still point to the universe as evidence for a creator-designer who is then identified with the scriptures' revelatory God. True, most theists speak of faith, yet that faith works alongside godly evidence. Indeed, theists often take umbrage when humanists describe faith as 'irrational leaping'.

Let us be clear here about the choice for theists. If faith involves adequate evidence, then it is right for that evidence to be assessed; and so humanists, such as Richard Dawkins, are correct in treating the belief that God exists as akin to a scientific hypothesis. If evidence is irrelevant, then what justifies a leap – or hop or skip – of faith? And in which direction to leap? Allah? The Christian God? The Devil?

Are all even numbers the sum of two prime numbers? One day, mathematicians may be able to justify, solely by reasoning, the correct answer. Does dark matter really exist? Perhaps astro-physicists will become more certain through empirical evidence. Does God exist? Some argue that the mere concept of God is sufficient to justify 'yes'. This argument is an ontological argument, touched on in Chapter 3. The argument is *a priori*, one independent of experience, in that it relies solely on reasoning about concepts. Most believers, more like scientists, turn to the *a posteriori*, to empirical experiences, arguing that the universe provides good evidence for God's existence. Main *a posteriori* arguments are versions of design and cosmological arguments, discussed in Chapter 2.

Explanatory accounts are usually of the causal or teleological variety. The car starting, the woman jogging – we readily assume that explanations can be offered: the car had a new battery; she was going to run a marathon. The new battery is involved in the causal explanation of the car's starting, whereas running a marathon – what the woman aimed at – is the end, the telos, which explains her jogging. Causes may be seen as pushes; ends sought as pulls. Causes come before the effects, metaphorically pushing the effects into existence. Ends sought, though, are in the future, metaphorically pulling the action, the jogging, into existence. Teleological explanations, these days, are reserved for human and other animals' behaviour. Earth does not orbit the sun because of some end in view.

Religious believers turn to a creator-designer, with purposes, with ends, to explain the universe's nature and existence. According to humanists, that is no good explanation at all, but akin to tales of planets moving with purposes in mind, to thunderbolts as divine interventions. Although ancient atomists rejected such teleological explanations, the rejection took no strong foothold until much later. Francis Bacon and Descartes, regarding non-human nature, sought the causal rather than teleological. It was Spinoza, a generation later, who pressed home objections to all teleological explanation, even of human behaviour, by two rhetorical questions. First, can we seriously explain what is happening *now* by something that occurs in the future – the end in view? Secondly, can we seriously explain what is happening now by something that may not even exist in the future? If a man jogs for health, health is the end – but he jogs because that end does not yet exist and he may, indeed, jog with futility, for that end may never come about. Health may evade him. There is, then, a difference between teleological explanations being wrong – moons do not orbit planets for a purpose – and teleological explanations being reducible to causal. The man really was jogging for his health, but arguably that means that his desire for health caused him to jog. We have, we may note, merely shifted the problem from how a future non-existent state can figure in an explanation to how it can be the object of a desire. The dust under the carpet that made an unsightly bump at the explanatory end has now been swept to the desire end.

Whatever style of explanation, the assumption is that things can be explained. Theists reach ultimately for a teleological explanation, with a causal mix: God caused the world to come into existence because of some divine end in view. Cosmological arguments stress the need for a cause; design arguments stress the designing. Fancy footwork is needed to identify creator with designer. Further, the existence of morality leads theists to ascribe moral agency to the creator-designer; and miracles and personal revelation point to the creator-designer's continuing concern for humans. Humanists are unimpressed with the arguments, individually and in combination. In so far as God is invoked in competition with scientific causal explanation, the scientific is preferred. In so far as God is used to provide teleological explanations of the universe, humanists see no need – as we shall see. For humanists, God is, so to speak, at best, an unneeded luxury without value, and, at worst, a great danger. We turn to the luxury.

2
Without God

If cattle and horses and lions had hands and could paint and make works of art with their hands just as people can, horses would depict the gods as horses and cattle would as cattle …

Xenophanes

Humanism and religion make a great fuss about God. In the end, were the fuss ever to end, the dispute hangs on where and when we should come to rest – come to rest, that is, in explanation. Should we be rested, or restless, with the thought that this just is how the universe is? If restless, does taking the step to God as explanation provide rest, even though we lack explanation of God's being just as he is? As Wittgenstein wrote, 'The difficulty here: is to stop.'

Belief in God is like belief in fairies – so say many humanists, though in Chapter 3, I shall suggest an alternative. Most humanists and theists understand 'belief in God' at least to include 'belief that God exists'. Belief in God involves an existential claim similar to those such as Robin Hood existed, fairies really do exist, and numbers have existence in an abstract realm. Many humanists and theists also understand belief in God, as in fairies, to require evidence. Absence of evidence is not the same as evidence of absence, but without some evidence – reasons, justifications – pointing to something, why would one think that the item in question existed?

Humanists' and theists' disagreement concerns the truth or falsity of the belief in God. For humanists, godly belief and fairy belief are alike in that, minimally, there is no good reason to hold them true. For theists, while there are no good reasons for thinking fairies exist, there are excellent reasons for thinking God exists. We are suppressing the caveats of 'most' and 'many'; in Chapter 3 we touch on those modern religious believers who understand belief in God radically differently from an existential belief, that is, from a straightforward belief that God *exists*.

Surprise

That the universe exists and exists as it does is a pleasant surprise for many. True, many of us may lament the universe, disappointed by worldly sufferings, our frailties and failures. Whether surprised by the universe's goodness, beauty and variety or its badness, ugliness and monotony, we remain surprised that this universe, as it is, exists. The surprise may centre on the varieties of life on earth, on the functionings of eyes and ears, hearts and brains. We may be amazed at the interdependence between species, environment and single cell organisms. The surprise is sometimes at the world's orderliness, at mathematical laws applying, or the presence of consciousness and morality. Such features are unlikely to have arisen by chance. To quell surprise, many explain that what appears unlikely is not unlikely at all. Heraclitus, a Greek philosopher of the fifth century BCE, argued that there must be a principle of reason underlying the universe. St John's Gospel speaks of the word – the logos, the reason – as being in the beginning. After all, when unlikely things happen in everyday experiences, we readily accept that explanations exist; we may simply not know what they are.

Why has something happened? Is it by chance? Is there an explanation in naturalistic terms of science? Must we resort to the supernatural? The latter three questions – Chance? Natural? Supernatural? – form our CNS questions. Why did the glass break? Well, there is a naturalistic explanation, maybe solely causal (the wind blew it), maybe partially teleological (to show her anger, she threw the ring at the window). Today we mostly assume that naturalistic explanations are available, though some still believe in godly interventions, perhaps by way of occasional miracles. But what of the big surprise, namely, the universe's existence? That anything exists at all is a surprise: it gives rise to cosmological arguments for God's existence. That what exists exists as it does gives rise to design arguments. To these arguments and humanism's rejection, we turn.

Design arguments abound. Going back many centuries, to the Indian Hindu Nyaya school, God's existence is argued for on the basis of kinship between artefacts and human bodies. In the Bible, Romans I, God's invisible qualities – his eternal power and divine nature – are seen clearly from what has been created. In eighteenth-century Britain, William Paley drew a famous analogy: walking on a heath, we come across a mechanical watch. Given the intricate mechanism, the wheels and springs functioning together, it would be irrational to accept that chance or natural laws alone account for its existence. Rather, we should believe in a designer, a being with a purpose; and we should believe this even if we discovered that watches replicated themselves, one being reproduced from an earlier. By analogy, there must be a designer of the universe: the universe contains intricate workings and interdependence of a magnificent array of creatures with organs that clearly serve functions. Overall, there are features and elements of the universe that resemble features and elements of humanly designed items. The resemblance is so strong that it is very, very likely that the universe is designed.

The argument hangs on the strength of the relevant similarities and lack of better alternative explanations. The watch–creature analogy, though, is weak. We can see how watches are manufactured, understand the physics involved, and we know what watches are meant to do. But we have no idea how a disembodied spirit could manufacture something. We have no idea what creatures are for. We have never beheld a disembodied spirit at work. This observational lack, as criticism, may, though, seem poor. Science postulates unobservable 'theoretical' entities, such as electrons and black holes, to explain observable events. With such suggested scientific entities, though, there is scope for confirmation or refutation: experiments can be conducted, predictions made, and hypotheses revised or rejected. No such testing applies to the God hypothesis.

For centuries the godly design explanation, however impoverished, was the best on offer. How else could one explain the existence of different species? Think of the CNS questioning. Chance? – highly implausible. Natural explanations? – unavailable. That leaves the supernatural 'S'. With scriptural support, many Christians held that the world and its species were created over six days around 4000 BCE, with God as designer. This is the 'creationist' explanation of the existence of the various species. Scriptures from other religions provide different accounts. Scriptural authority of any kind, however happened upon, is now no longer needed. A naturalistic explanation is available; yet surprisingly – and to humanists' distress – cosmic design tales remain popular, either through traditional creationist theory or the (allegedly new) idea of intelligent design or 'fine-tuning'.

Created splashes

We may think of species as splashes of variety for which creationists give praise to a designing creator. Humanists give praise to Charles Darwin. Darwin, once an avid reader of Paley, showed the way whereby what may appear designed can be explained as non-designed.

The eyes' functioning *seems* to have been designed to enable us to see and to coordinate with other perceptions. Eyes, of course, as theists and humanists agree, come about through causal developments, fertilization of ovum, leading to growth of foetus and so on; but what is the explanation for that complex reproductive mechanism existing at all? Must it not have been designed? These metaphorical splashes of variety and complexity – of human beings and other creatures – intrigue us. Presumably, though, had there existed solely one self-sustaining animal species, there would still have been theoretical bafflement at its existence.

Although others, including the ancient Greeks, had suggested evolutionary theories, until Darwin such theories lacked much support. Darwin's evolutionary theory (more accurately, theories of natural selection and sexual selection) contained many gaps, but he judged correctly that the gaps would be filled. That there is variation in offspring, with the variation, if beneficial to survival or reproduction, being passed to subsequent offspring, is now understood through genetic theory. Fossils of transitional life-forms, of graduated diversities, have recently been discovered. Darwin's theory, furthermore, has the virtue of being open to refutation: if, for example, we somehow showed that complex biological organs could not be formed through slight modifications over generations, then the theory would be rightly questioned. For such reasons as presence of evidence, prediction of future discoveries, and explanatory fit with other scientific theories, Darwin's theory, suitably modified by genetics, is a vastly better theory than a vague, untestable hand wave towards an unknown godly designer courtesy of selected scriptural stories.

Darwin presents natural selection as analogous to domestic selection: it is a better analogy than Paley's watch–creature analogy. Humans have selectively bred animals over generations, with different-looking animals resulting: just consider the different hounds and horses in *Horse and Hound*. Such variation results from domestication. Darwin viewed nature as engaged metaphorically in selective breeding.

The key idea is that the seeming improbability of the huge complexity of life results from numerous very small and simple changes in organisms, with selection favouring some over others: that is, some survive and flourish at the expense of others, the survivors producing more offspring which are largely good copies, though some with further small variations that offer the possibility of additional improved adaptation. Physical causes alone, over billions of years, have led to the appearance of complex design. Reflect that an extremely complex colour image may yet consist of millions of pixels, each of which is composed of three simples, red, green and blue.

Humanism, therefore, has a good scientific, causal theory to replace the creationist, teleological hand wave – a theory that draws attention to just how unscientific is the creationist alternative. The creationist alternative fails to mesh with concepts of other theories. In contrast with evolutionary genetic explanation, creationism fails to explain adequately the dating of fossils, the inefficiencies of some organs – and so forth. Creationists must doubt much of the scientific theory that leads to current beliefs concerning geological dating and formation of the solar system. Once such are doubted, why believe creation occurred fewer than ten thousand years ago? The answer is that the belief relies on a selection of certain scriptures – that is, on past wild speculations. Once the selected scriptural authority is removed, and the empirical evidence ignored, we could equally well suggest that the universe was designed and created just five minutes ago – a sceptical suggestion by Bertrand Russell – with all our seeming memories, biblical records and schedules of television programmes. Or six minutes ago; or seven – and so on ...

The rejection of creationism has largely been brought about by the success of evolutionary theory; the rejection, though, should not depend on that success. Creationism was a poor theory even when there was no evolutionary alternative. A bad theory is not better than no theory.

Humanists sometimes give the impression that evolutionary theory has the final say about human development. There are, though, criticisms. No convincing explanation yet exists of how our experiences relate to the physical world and their evolutionary value. It may be that the development of psychological features – of consciousness, desires, beliefs, sensations – cannot be accounted for in concepts of current science and causal laws, but require teleological laws of some kind, perhaps in terms of 'functioning for'. Humanists impressed by current scientific theory should remember how radically scientific understanding can change. No one a hundred years ago foresaw the development of quantum mechanics.

None of the above suggests that a reference to God will pop up in future scientific explanations. None of the above suggests that we should have patience with the silly idea that evolutionary theory is 'just a theory' on a par with any creationist theory plucked from scripture. Evolutionary theory is a group of propositions that explains an enormous amount: it figures in epidemiology, genetics and breeding. It no more deserves to be dismissed as 'just a theory' than theories which explain planetary motions. Newtonian theory was superseded by Einsteinian, but that does not place Newtonian mechanics on a par with astrological, homeopathic or 'crystal ball gazing' theories. Newtonian mechanics remains highly valuable and much used.

Current evolutionary theory requires the existence of complex molecules carrying genetic information – DNA – molecules that replicate, mutate and give rise to different organisms. We may, therefore, reasonably enquire how such material came about. Evolutionary theory does not answer *that*. This provides design theorists with hope. Hope is, though, dangerous; it often leads to disappointment. At best, this hope is for God being necessary for the existence of a universe which gives rise to such complex molecules. So, while many – atheists and theists alike – accept that evolutionary theory has rid us of the need for a godly designer of species, the theory does not quell surprise at the existence of a universe with its evolutionary mechanism.

So, let us move to the bigger splash – the splash of the whole universe, a universe once likened by Robert Boyle to the Great Clock of Strasbourg – a splash, once again, allegedly pointing to a designer. Creationists will, of course, simply insist that the Bible (or other favoured scripture) tells us when this happened, courtesy of God. Supporters of intelligent fine-tuning, though, are happy to accept current scientific claims about the universe, for example, developing from a big bang, billions of years ago, but insist that an explanation referring to God as cause and designer is still required.

A bigger splash, intelligently and finely tuned?

There seem to be many, many, many ways a universe could be. Indeed, there is an infinite number of ways; an infinite number of possible universes. The whole universe could have been a place with no life at all. Maybe it could have been a place with only hydrogen. Whatever the laws of nature actually are, whatever physicists claim to have discovered about them, they might not have been so – well, that is how it seems. Logical contradictions, for example, that there is a square circle, cannot possibly be the case, but, those to one side, it looks as if anything could have been the case. How surprising, then, that the existent world does contain the things it does, in particular the complexes of life; of trees and butterflies and warm beer – of cricket and romance and ballet. It seems extremely unlikely to have come about by chance. Whatever the natural evolutionary explanations of little splashes of species in harmony (the harmony of eating each other, we may note), they afford no explanation for the whole set-up, the world, the universe.

One thing true of the universe is that it supports life. More specifically, at least one teeny part of the universe is such that, for some small period of time, life exists. If there be a cosmic life builder, he looks to be something of a dubious jerry-builder, given the fragility and scarcity of that life. Although 'life' is the term used by many when identifying the universe's surprising feature, what really surprises is – well, it is not clear quite what is meant to be surprising. Often the surprise is at the enormous complexity and variety involved in life; often it is linked specifically to human beings, to consciousness, intelligence, beliefs, aims and emotions. Sometimes it is surprise at the sheer improbability of the specificity of the universe's features that give rise to life existing. Sometimes it is the existence of those features that do indeed give rise to life. Of course, earthworms and bacteria and viruses are also pretty complex, as are many other structures. Whether just their existence would lead believers to claim that God would have to have existed, who knows? Let us stick to being surprised at the existence of conscious intelligent beings able to perceive, reflect and act – at the existence of people.

We, conscious beings, exist. So, of course, the universe is such a place that conscious beings exist; but it may still be surprising that the universe *is* such a place. When in flight on aeroplanes, we should not be surprised at our being able to *conclude* that Earth is a planet that sustains flight; but we may still be surprised that Earth is such a planet. A classic example making the same point is: you are before a firing squad. The squad fires, intent on killing you – yet you remain alive. It is unsurprising that you can conclude that they all missed; you are still alive, so obviously they all missed. It remains extremely surprising that they missed. Surprise at this universe existing is encouraged by the thought that conscious life could come into existence only if the various features of this universe existed more or less as they do; the features seem 'finely tuned' to bring humans into existence.

The above aeroplane and firing squad examples are sometimes cloaked in an unkindly confusion of anthropic principles: anthropoi are humans; 'principle' suggests something grandiose. One such principle is benign, uninteresting and weak; another is interesting, strong, but not benign. Weak versions are: 'What we may expect to observe must be restricted by the conditions necessary for our presence as observers,' and 'We should expect to discover laws of nature compatible with the existence of human observers.' We should certainly expect the compatibility, but the particular laws that we find present may not be necessary for our presence. Benignly, we may infer that the total conditions around us are sufficient for our existence – and whatever conditions are necessary for our existence are within that totality – but it follows from this neither that *all* the conditions around us are necessary for our existence nor that there may not be other conditions (not happening to exist) such that, were they to exist and supplement the necessary ones, they would be sufficient for our existence.

The weak anthropic principle in no way explains the universe's existence, so it is curious that some humanists apparently regard it as an alternative to creator-designer explanations, quelling surprise. Dawkins, for example, uses it to quell our surprise at the Earth's friendliness to life, commenting, 'however small the minority of planets with just the right conditions for life may be, we necessarily have to be on one of that minority, because here we are thinking about it'. Martin Rees, now Lord Rees, writes that the universe's hugeness 'which seems at first to signify how unimportant we are in the cosmic scheme, is actually entailed by our existence' and 'shouldn't surprise us, even though we may still seek a deeper explanation of its distinctive features.' Both scientists, though, recognize, in the end, that the benign anthropic principle fails to meet the godly challenge based on the unlikeliness of the universe.

The strong anthropic principle comes in different versions. One version is that only very specific features of a universe would give rise to conscious life; another version is that the very specific features of this universe had to give rise to conscious life; and, sometimes, there is an addition, namely the bizarre claim that such life will never die out. Sometimes the strong principle is simply that the universe seems finely tuned or even is finely tuned. Of course, the latter strong principle quickly leads to the claim that there is a being that did the fine-tuning.

The puzzle is the fact that our universe possesses features that give rise to conscious life, given that the universe could have been different in an infinite number of ways, without conscious life. Rees identifies six numbers as the 'recipe' for a universe, involving basic forces, texture and space. If any one were 'untuned', there would be no life. We perhaps should not be so impressed by these details. Juggling different combinations of changes in constants may, for all we know, produce conscious life. Further, scientists continue to revise their understanding of fundamental laws. Further still, there remains bafflement over how consciousness relates to the physical world. Even with those doubts, it may still appear surprising that the existent universe is one of the few that gives rise to conscious life. Our CNS questions come to the fore. Chance? But it just is so incredibly unlikely. Naturalist explanation? No plausible one exists. We are driven to the supernatural, to God – or so theists, the defenders of versions of intelligent design or fine-tuning, believe.

The theist claim is that the universe is vastly more probable under the God hypothesis than under the 'no God'. If, though, God is identified solely as whatever *caused* the universe, we retain mystery: we have either the mystery of why such a being *happens* to exist or why a necessarily existent being gives rise to this particular universe. We have made no explanatory progress. The godly hypothesis comes to bear the explanatory load because of its teleological nature. The universe's features point allegedly to an intelligent designer who designs for a purpose. Maybe conscious life is valuable; this indicates a designer who is good, creating items of value. Even within this approach, humanists may fairly challenge. If the universe has been designed for conscious life, why is there so little? If it is so valuable that conscious life should exist, why has it arisen through evolutionary processes that might not have resulted in such life? There are further objections.

Dawkins' objection, a typical humanist objection, is that the designer would need to possess at least as much complexity as the universe; hence, the explanation is no explanation at all. The reply is that the intelligent designer is an intentional being, not a vast collection of physical particles. We do possess a grip on how intentions and aims may be simple, yet give rise to physical complexity. Complex means may be made intelligible by simple aims. Further, the typical general humanist objection, that we still require an explanation of God, does not address the theistic claim that the universe is evidence of a designer. Singing and staggering may point to philosophers being drunk, even if it remains a mystery why they are drunk.

None of this implies that all is well with the postulation of the intelligent designer. For a start, what sense can be made of *disembodied* intentional agency, why just one agency and why the identification with (for example) the God of the New Testament? Even if sense can be made of such agency, have we made explanatory progress, if the problem is that of explaining unlikeliness? Whatever the designer's aims, they may be as unlikely as the existence of this particular universe.

The believers' response is sometimes the simple insistence that the universe sports evidence of fine-tuning; and fine-tuning points to a designer. This is in tension with the earlier design argument of creationism: there, the existence of the different species is seen as so surprising and out of tune, given the universe's laws, that there must have been direct divine creation of species. A similar tension arises between those many theists who have been impressed by the world's orderliness, and those keen to explain the world's disorderliness through (alleged)

HUMANIST HUME – AND W. C. FIELDS

David Hume (1711–1776) is a humanist dream. He set the Enlightenment humanist tone, questioning God's existence and the value of religion with fine argument, irony and good humour.

Throughout his life, Hume was excellent company, recognizing the fellow feeling we typically have. When he visited the French Enlightenment sceptics, he quipped that he had been unable to believe in the existence of atheists – until in Paris. When arguing against belief in miracles, he ended up reflecting ironically that maybe there is the one great miracle, namely, that people believe in miracles. When examining design arguments for God's existence, he mused that many items are designed by committees or apprentices, so we could conclude that a divine committee or rude infant apprentices probably designed the universe: maybe this universe is the first botched attempt of an infant deity.

On his death-bed, people waited for him to recant and pray to God. He did not.

W. C. Fields, the American actor-comedian and life-long atheist, was found reading the Bible, when nearing his end. Friends asked whether he was converting. 'No,' replied Fields, 'just looking for loopholes.' Hume would have approved the humour.

miracles. To be fair, we ought not to cast some believers as inconsistent because other believers hold beliefs inconsistent with the former's. It is striking, though, how believers in the same God apparently see the world around them so differently from each other. Perhaps this is itself a small contribution to the world's variety.

Recently, naturalistic contenders for explaining the seeming fine-tuning have come to the fore. There is a Darwinian type of approach, suggesting that many, many worlds randomly came about, with different laws of nature, and some, so to speak, evolved into our universe. That our universe eventually came to exist should not surprise, given so many others have existed.

Another idea, with historical precedents, is that, as time is infinite and maybe matter is finite, there are oscillations between big bang, expansion, contraction and crunch, with random variation in the constants each time round leading to different natural laws. Hence, many, many variations come around; and it is unsurprising that this variation supporting conscious life has come around. A third version, for example from Rees, is the existence of an infinity of different universes, isolated from each other, with different natural laws.

All three are attempts to show that our universe is not unlikely. This is because all the other possible universes do exist or get their turn to exist. Apart from potential for terminological confusion – after all, 'universe' usually covers everything except God – all three ideas have dubious moves in reasoning and raise questions of what evidence there could be for them.

What else is on offer for the humanists to answer intelligent design? Some may be swept along by physicists' talk of a Theory of Everything being on the horizon, but that is exaggerated talk for the thought that maybe a unifying law of nature will be discovered. We should still be surprised why the unified law that led to conscious life existed rather than another.

If we doubt the recent scientific attempts to explain the universe as likely, must we be driven back to some version of intelligent design through fine-tuning?

We need not be driven – and should not be. My humanistic recommendation is that we should resist the lure of explanatory expectations. One 'no explanation required' view is that it does not make sense to speak of possibilities, probabilities and necessities when we are speaking of the total universe (hereafter back with its traditional meaning of everything that exists, save God). With a throw of a fair die, we have both the intuitive *a priori* conception of there being six possible outcomes, equally likely, and empirical evidence of how there tends, indeed, to be equal frequency of those outcomes. But when we have only the one universe, what sense can be made of the frequency of universes, or of the propensities of different universes towards existence, or of the equiprobability of different outcomes?

Let us pretend, though, that we do have a clear idea of different possible universes and of how this is one very unlikely universe. Here is a final 'no explanation required' approach.

Simply, surprising things happen. A lottery winner is usually surprised; the win is, say, one chance in fourteen million. In this case, we have an explanation. The games are designed such that someone will win, but it is unlikely that the particular individual wins. We believe the outcome is causally determined, but we lack knowledge of many relevant factors. This contrasts with decaying uranium; currently it is believed that it is not determined which portions decay first. Unlikely things happen; indeed, in these cases, it is very likely (even certain) that unlikely things will happen. It is, paradoxically, a mistake to think that unlikely things are unlikely.

Assuming this universe is one of an infinite number of possible universes, *whichever* existed would be immensely unlikely. Now, in an infinite number of them as opposed to all – 'infinite' differs from 'all': an infinite number of numbers, say, the even numbers, does not amount to all the numbers – there would be no conscious beings to be surprised, but any particular universe would still be incredibly unlikely and would have generated surprise, had, *per impossibile*, conscious beings been present. A universe that consisted mainly of pebbles, or unknown gases, or was much like ours, save life only reaches the amoeba stage, would be (so to speak) distinctive to the pebbles, gases or amoeba; metaphorically, they could propose cosmic designers or artists: some minimalist in preference, akin to a Barnet Newman or Mark Rothko; some more chaotic, akin to a Jackson Pollock. Intelligent design theorists, though, apply their approach to this particular universe alone, thinking only this one, or very similar, would call out for a designing account. That is irrational. We may be tempted to say, with the epigram from Xenophanes in mind, that because only humans design, many believe only our universe merits a designer. If we accept that any universe that existed would be distinctive in its way, then an argument for God's existence on empirical grounds becomes an argument on the basis that something exists at all, whatever structure or so-called design it has. And this moves us to cosmological arguments for the existence of God. We could, though, simply rest with the thought that something unlikely would have happened, whatever happened; and that is where we stop.

Mystery

Belief that there must be a sufficient reason for everything is, according to Leibniz, the apex of rationality. Apply the belief to the universe, be it a multiverse or not, be it seemingly manifesting design or not: we must infer to God who caused or grounds the universe – or so many theists claim. Many times has this argument, a cosmological argument, been propounded from pubs to mosques to philosophy classes. In basic versions, the argument is dreadful. It usually reads 'reasons' as causes, asserting that everything must have a cause. It then provides the picture of a temporal sequence of events, one event having been caused by a previous one, with a first cause at the beginning that is duly identified as God. But that accepts that God lacks a cause, hence undermining the premiss that everything has a cause.

Leibniz explicitly avoids the above mistake. What needs to be explained, for Leibniz, is not present in what he postulates to do the explaining. The sequences of events making up the universe are contingent: they just happen to be. To postulate a first cause to explain such happenings achieves nothing, if that first cause also just happens to be. Indeed, Leibniz accepts that the sequences may go back infinitely, without beginning. The only reason sufficient to explain the existence of contingent things is something that necessarily exists, namely, God.

Humanists see this argument as generating mystery rather than explanation. Some may be content to settle for the universe being infinitely extended in time, with no beginning and no end. Explanations have to come to an end; states of the universe do not. William Wollaston, however, in his early eighteenth-century work, supposed a chain hanging from heaven, the explanation why any link does not crash groundward being that it is held securely by the next link up – and so on. Yet, asks Wollaston, is that satisfactory, for whenever an explanation is given, the question arises again. Mind you, we may comment, whenever the question arises again, a further explanation can be given. Maybe the best that can be said is that we have to stop questioning. Wollaston, though, seeks an explanation for the existence of the whole chain's hanging. But what answer could satisfy him, save the claim that there is a self-holding body that holds the chain – but what can that be? May it not just be the mysterious chain? Of course, Wollaston uses the chain analogy to lead us to God as the being that supports the universe.

What is achieved by insisting that the universe was created, or is supported, by a necessarily existing being? If necessary existence makes sense, maybe the universe just is such a necessary existent, even if elements within it are contingent. Further, if God is necessarily existent, eternal, outside time – often also said to be simple and unchanging – how can he be creator of anything; how, indeed, can contingent items derive from what is necessary?

Sometimes the thought is that God's necessary existence closes down questions concerning his existence; but it should not. We may wonder why there exists such a being at all as well as whether and how the putative necessity flows from other features of God. If theists settle for mysteries here, as seems inevitable, then we may as well settle for no explanation for the universe's existence, leaving out the divine mystery supplement. Things are not helped by adding that God should be understood as the 'condition of our being' or the 'condition of the possibility of any entity'; for what exactly does that mean, why think there must be a condition, and how does it link to the personal God worshipped by millions?

★   ★   ★

This chapter has skimmed the surfaces of arguments for God's existence. There are many subtleties: doubts over evolutionary explanations, if no intelligence or teleology within; deeper investigations into possible worlds, probabilities and causation. For humanists, two basic challenges to religious believers hold fast. First, if the universe's existence is a mystery, how is that mystery resolved by introducing another being – God – whose existence is a mystery? If it is, though, insisted that God possesses features that show his existence to lack mystery, then my reply is that maybe the universe possesses those features and hence there is no need to postulate another being, namely, God, to avoid mystery. Secondly, even if arguments point to a creator-designer, they go no way towards showing that the creator-designer possesses the many attributes ascribed in scriptures to God.

Religion very much has a practical import: on how believers live their lives – yet the detailed religious recipes for living cannot be convincingly derived from metaphysical arguments for a divine creator-designer, even were those arguments convincing. It is to the practical import that we now turn.

3
Without religion

The critique of religion disenchants man so that he should think, act, and shape his reality like a man who, disenchanted, has regained reason, that he should move around himself and thus around his true sun. Religion is only the illusory sun that moves around man as long as he does not move around himself.

Karl Marx

There is something odd about God; perhaps there is something sensible and good about religions. Perhaps religions provide us with valuable ways of looking at the world, even if belief in an existent God is literally false. False beliefs can generate valuable outcomes; witness the placebo effect. *Belief* that the pills will make you better may make you better; it is the belief that is sometimes effective, not the pills. Of course, believing that God exists does not make God exist; but it may have beneficial consequences. Perhaps religions hold societies together, promote flourishing lives and sustain morality. Religions may achieve these things, even with God absent. Perhaps the godly belief should simply be defended on grounds of utility: it generates certain valuable attitudes and actions; it encourages a reverence towards the world, towards others and, indeed, towards oneself. Well, it can do – and often does.

Sometimes the distinctive feature of religion is marked by stressing belief *in* God, rather than belief *that* God exists. Belief in God is suggestive more of trust, but that does not remove belief that God exists; an individual's existence is presupposed when placing trust in that individual. Most religious believers do not see their religion solely in terms of its value here on earth; a very few do. At this chapter's end, we turn to the few – the few who drop the ontological claim that God really exists.

We shall focus on the frequent and confident religious assertion that God, or at least belief in God, is necessary for morality. Of course, religious belief typically embraces more than the ontological claim that God exists; it may include, for example, that God is Love and that Christ is the Son. The usual arguments for a creator-designer in no way justify these luxury extras. They derive, for most believers, from scripture.

Dangerous faith

'Are you, dear religious believers, really saying that if you lacked belief in God, then you'd feel free to rape, torture and murder whenever you wanted? Is it solely God's commandments that make such actions immoral?' That is the basic humanist challenge. Caveats and squirms are needed, but at heart the reply is either 'no', suggesting that religion is unnecessary, or 'yes', suggesting that these believers are pretty immoral and nasty characters – and best to have no truck with them.

Moral truths concern what it is right and wrong to do and what are good and bad outcomes. They are also manifest in more discerning assessments, for example, those involving justice, courage and benevolence. With all such matters, we tussle over what we morally ought or ought not to do or how things ought or ought not to be; we may speak of duties and rights, of virtues and vices. Exactly how such judgements intermesh is a formidable question; but, here, we need merely to consider how morality generally stands with regard to God and belief in God. It should be noted that use of 'good' and 'bad' does not necessarily involve moral judgements. 'Their movements on stage are good, but their singing is bad' raises matters of aesthetics, not of morality.

> ### 'PRIESTS AND CONJURERS ARE OF THE SAME TRADE'
>
> Thomas Paine (1737–1809), an Anglo-American free-thinker, fought hard against the immoralities and conjuring tricks of scriptures, faith and religious institutions. Whether Jewish, Christian or Turkish, they 'appear to me no other than human inventions, set up to terrify and enslave mankind, and monopolize power and profit.'
>
> Paine relied on humanity, on the Religion of Humanity – a term he introduced which was used later, in the nineteenth century, in different ways by Auguste Comte and John Stuart Mill. For Paine, it was a commitment to reason and fellow feeling.
>
> 'When I contemplate the natural dignity of man; when I feel … for the honour and happiness of its character, I become irritated at the attempt to govern mankind by force and fraud, as if they were all knaves and fools …'
>
> With this humanist approach, he sought the end of the slave trade, fought for equal rights, and spoke up for free speech.

That morality depends on belief in God is not an unusual claim. In the eighteenth century, Jean-Jacques Rousseau – well known, if only for misogyny and forcing people to be free (see Chapter 8) – asserted society's need for a few basic religious dogmas, a need that could justify the death penalty for proclaimed atheists. In the same century, the Reverend Conyers Middleton – a man little known in all respects – writes of how, even if Christianity is an imposture, it is built into law, has a long tradition and could not be replaced by reason. Later, in the nineteenth century, we find Matthew Arnold, in his poem 'Dover Beach', regretting people's loss of faith: the Sea of Faith, 'its melancholy, long, withdrawing roar, retreating'. Many people – politicians, parents, among others – continue today to believe that moral behaviour requires, and results from, a religious education. Humanists argue that the religion-morality connection is both mistaken and morally dangerous, generating irrationality, superstition and intolerance.

Whether belief in God possesses moral benefits may be an empirical question, one to be investigated by looking at the facts. In contrast with that question, there are conceptual questions involving morality, belief in God and, indeed, God. Whatever the connections, one fundamental problem is the source and content of the religious beliefs: much that is proclaimed by the religious merits the retort, 'It ain't necessarily so.' Here are two simple questions. Which religion? Which claims? To insist that morality, and even fundamental claims about the world, are grounded in religion and nothing else is glib. It merits humanistic ironic laughter tinged with despair at the horrors committed in God's name. Numerous religious claims conflict with each other; hence, they cannot all be true. Even within a particular model or brand of a particular religion, there are conflicts, unless nifty footwork occurs in the interpretative free dance. The footwork often occurs.

Many religious claims are factually false. We can tell this because some claims contradict others. Within the Bible there is conflict about the order of creation; inconsistent accounts exist of Christ's life; and, once we bring the Qur'an and other scriptures into the frame, we have a mish-mash of tales, taking us from burning bushes to God's making a mortal woman pregnant to the existence of mixed angels. We may wonder why some ancient texts secure the aura of special authority, whereas others do not. Immense authority is often ascribed to one particular text that believers live by: 'The Book'. For humanism, that is a dismissal of rationality. Humanists have books. They assess evidence, reasons, justifications; they subscribe uncritically to no 'The Book'.

Many believers accept that scripture is sometimes factually mistaken. To put it pithily, following the sixteenth-century

Cardinal Baronius, the Bible tells us not how the heavens go, but how to go to heaven. Scripture should be read for the *prescriptive*, with what is morally required, not for descriptive history. Humanists happily agree that scriptures are unreliable sources for empirical facts; humanists, though, also consider them unreliable regarding morality. Of course, some moral injunctions in religious texts merit humanistic agreement; many do not. 'Do unto others as you would have them do unto you' is a scriptural injunction valued by humanists; such a golden rule existed long before the earthly life of Jesus Christ. Humanists insist that religion is not required in order to recognize the morality involved in such an injunction. Furthermore, even those moral injunctions, suitably interpreted, that do merit agreement do not do so *because* of their scriptural basis.

Pope Osama bin Laden – and a missing page

The outrageous heading is to startle and draw attention to a strong humanist point. Once morality is based upon interpretation of scripture – or indeed personal 'divine' revelation – severe danger lurks. Think of the AIDs suffering indirectly resulting from Catholic prohibitions on artificial contraception. Think of various Islamic–inspired threats to wipe out the Jews. It is but self-deception when politicians optimistically assert that 'true' Islam advocates living peacefully with Christians and Jews. No doubt many Muslims do; but many do not. Further, *even if* all religions happened to have compatible scriptures advocating peace, love and harmony, there would remain the risk of other individuals, one day, defending non-harmonious living on the basis of new aggressive religions. Hanging the label 'religion' round a set of beliefs, however sincerely held, however ancient the texts they are founded upon, does not make them respectable.

Humanists have field days when they read the scriptures and inspired words of religious authorities, from popes to imams to vicars. There is a god-intoxicated chaos of injunctions that vary both between religions and within a single religion, leading to incompatibilities and some downright immoralities parading as moral. For example, children, the Bible tells us, should not be put to death for their father's sins: well, that's a relief. Hold on; elsewhere the Lord orders some children to be prepared for slaughter because of their father's sins. True, some believers insist that all believers worship the same God, with the same core moral values, but it is difficult to identify any core values being consistently upheld by the different religions, not least when we consider the eagerness of various religious groups to be 'cleansed' of others.

Theists may insist that the above criticisms involve misunderstanding the true voice of God. 'Yes, misreading scriptures can have bad outcomes, but,' they say, 'humanism misses a vital point: morality is conceptually tied to God's existence. God ordains what is right and wrong – and we discover what is right and wrong from a proper understanding of the true scriptures.' It is to those claims that we turn.

Do religious beliefs overall generate good behaviour? No one really knows. What, though, is the conceptual or logical link between morality and God's existence and belief in God? Humanists claim that there is none – well, none in an interesting way. Theists typically disagree: what is right is dependent on God, perhaps in the way that what is triangular is dependent on straight sides. Humanists reply that what makes killing wrong does not hang on God, but on life's value. Theists respond that life has value only because it is God's gift. Humanists counter that killing is still wrong, even though life is not godly given.

Humanists argue not merely that belief in God is unnecessary for someone consistently to uphold morality, but also that moral concepts *cannot* be conceptually grounded in God as an all-powerful commander. There is fallacy in thinking that they can. True, if God is required for the existence of everything, obviously he is required for morality's existence. True, if God necessarily is good, then there may be a conceptual link between God and such goodness. The interesting question, though, is whether morality, simply in virtue of being morality, requires the existence of a divine being. A common religious claim, for example, is that what counts as morally good is logically determined by God's commands. Here is a small story of such commands, courtesy of a missing page. Humanists may then use the story to challenge the claimed link between morality and God.

Consider some sincere Christian evangelicals who seemingly ground their moral beliefs in close biblical readings. Suppose discovery of a missing page of Christ's teachings, a page with the same historical source as the gospels. On this page, Christ is clearly reported as saying, near the end of his life, that many of his early parables are likely to be misunderstood; hence, he is making it as clear as possible that God's teachings really do mean giving up one's wealth to help the dispossessed, welcoming all strangers into one's home, and the stoning of all those engaged in 'unnatural' sexual activities. How would the evangelicals respond?

Many would interpret the page to cohere with their existing moral beliefs and what their conscience tells them – the *interpretation* tactic. They may argue about what is meant by 'wealth' and 'dispossessed', how 'home' is 'home of the heart' rather than physical property and, well, as for 'unnatural', what should be counted as that? Some, by contrast, may take the words as literally as possible, but claim to know that God would not make such demands as the stoning, so the page must be fake – the *rejection* tactic. Both of those imply an *independence* assumption; they have prior moral beliefs independently of what is written on the page. Some of the believers, of course, may just accept the page's word, literally taken – though even here they would need some prior views about the nature of the 'unnatural'. The acceptance possibility illustrates, bearing in mind the page's stoning injunction, the danger that we have already spotted. It also suggests *motivational* puzzles, discussed further below. We turn first though to the humanist response, bearing in mind the story's reference to interpretation, rejection and independence approaches.

The missing page, as with religious texts and revelations, would no doubt generate argument. Such possible and actual arguments provide fuel for the humanist rejection of reliance on scripture as God's word, in determining morality. The humanist focus is on the basis of the theists' assessment of the missing page – and scriptures more generally. The basis must involve prior moral commitments. 'As God is good,' many theists would implicitly reason, 'and goodness involves not harming people, the missing page's stoning recommendation needs special interpretation or rejection.' Such interpretation or rejection is, indeed, a frequent theist approach, when encountering unacceptable scriptural injunctions. This suggests, though not conclusively, that theists have an understanding of what is right and wrong, independently of what scriptures say and God commands. It also shows that God does not speak clearly or, if he does, he does not enable vast numbers properly to hear. That alone raises some doubts about God's goodness.

That some religious believers, from different faiths, pick and match their texts, seeking a common core, also suggests that there are pre-existing moral beliefs, standing independently of particular scriptures. There is the religious' response to this criticism, the response that the pre-existing moral beliefs were handed down through generations, yet ultimately sourced in religious authority. While the handing down is largely the case, the 'ultimate source' assumption is false. People have held recognizable moralities without relying on scriptural authority.

Further, what has been found morally acceptable has changed over the centuries, sometimes for the better – and the changes have led to new scriptural interpretations.

The humanist argument concerning interpretation and rejection shows that theists – well, at least many – possess a grasp of what is right and wrong independently of any scriptures; indeed, it is that independent grasp that enables them to judge whether what the scriptures recommend is right or wrong. However, we have not yet shown that what *constitutes* being right and wrong is not grounded in God. Theists sometimes tell us that what makes something right simply is that God commands it. This theist claim can be challenged by an argument derived from Plato's treatment of piety in his *Euthyphro*; it has been much promoted by humanists. The challenge covers two questions: why we should accept God's commands as morally good; and why God commands whatever it is that he commands.

If moral goodness just is what God commands, then whatever God commands would be good. Now, suppose God commands stoning, torture or the killing of those who wear size ten shoes: would such actions thereby be elements of goodness? Certainly not. And our recognition of that point shows that what is good is not a matter of what God commands. The authority of God needs independent assessment and, given that need, for him, in that respect, we have no need. It is as simple as that.

Yet it is not as simple as that. Chemists discovered that water is H_2O. As water is H_2O, can something be water and yet not be H_2O? Some suggest that water *necessarily* is H_2O, even though we may never have known this and, when not knowing this, we could sensibly think that water is not H_2O. Similarly, some may suggest that being good is necessarily identical with being commanded by God, even though we may erroneously think them distinct. However, even if this is a possible analysis of what it is to be good, it does not follow that it holds true; indeed, we have some evidence that goodness is not identical with God's commands, for scriptures, allegedly telling of God's commands, often command immoral deeds – yet suppose the scriptures are largely mistaken. Suppose that God has not commanded immoral deeds such as the slaughter of the Egyptian firstborn, but does always command only what is good. Maybe the water analogy now holds. Conceiving of God's commands as distinct from the good does not show that they are not identical, necessarily identical, indeed. The humanist rejection of goodness as identical with what God commands is not – dare I say? – watertight.

We may reply by turning to the second question. Why is it that God commands something? Presumably, it is because that something is good; but if goodness just is whatever God commands, then to judge that God is good amounts to no more than that God commands whatever he commands – hardly an impressive reason for praising God – and God's motivation towards goodness is but a motivation to do anything. Once again, we have an argument showing that morality is independent of God. It is as simple as that.

Once again, it is not that simple. In praising God some may simply be valuing goodness rather than praising a divine agent who commands the good. However, the thought that it is goodness itself which is being praised – with God simply being goodness – moves us away from typical theist beliefs in a personal God who creates, loves and judges; or, at least, it demands some explanation of God's nature.

The overall humanist stance is that moral behaviour needs neither God nor belief in God nor the motivation to please God. To be aware of what one morally ought to do does not require belief that God exists or belief in certain scriptures as divinely inspired. It is not merely that, as a matter of fact, theists often do interpret or reject scriptures according to their independently held morality; it is what they *ought* to do. They ought to evaluate whether particular so-called godly commands are morally right; and that evaluation should be independent of the so-called commands. This is not to suggest that the humanist stance is without puzzlement, for we may be tempted to think some explanation is required of the basis for any moral evaluations.

Turning to motivation, that something is commanded by God ought not to be the motivation for doing what is morally right. Humanists rightly point out that, *if* that is the motivation, then one danger is that, if or when people cease to believe in God, their morality loses all grounding. Another danger is that the motivation may be tied up with self-interest: believers seem to do what is taken to be morally right because of heavenly rewards. We may, of course, wonder how strong a draw is the nebulous heavenly prospect; after all, theists rarely think that fear of hell is sufficient to dispense with locked doors and laws against theft. None the less heavenly self-interest often does feature in religious texts and sermons commending moral behaviour.

Suppose a celebrity helps the homeless by volunteer work, a good thing to do. In that respect, she is a good person. Or is she? Suppose that she volunteers solely because she wants to be seen as charitable, boosting her public image. Although something good gets done, it is far from obvious that she is acting morally, that she is of good character. Rather, she is acting out of self-interest. Such motivational moral meanness applies to some religious believers. Many believers are encouraged to perform their good deeds on the basis of improved heavenly chances. This undermines their moral standing. True, good things get done, but not, in that respect, by good people. Theists may reply that the heavenly rewards are only foreseen, not primarily intended; the believers would perform their good deeds, even without godly belief. If so, then again we see how moral action is not grounded – or, at least, not obviously grounded – in belief in God.

Heavenly virgins, belief and commitment

Whether the number be seventy-two and whether they be nubile female virgins or white raisins – there is, I understand, a Qur'an translational question, the outcome of which could lead to grave disappointments – the ends sought, through religiously inspired actions, may also raise motivational questions. Why would suicide bombers – seen as martyrs – bomb innocent people? Well, if they have prior belief in God and his rewards and punishments, the calculation may be obvious: loss of earthly life, an earthly life perhaps of much toil and hardship, compared with an immediate eternal afterlife of an especially appealing, sensual ilk. Thrown into the calculation would need to be the likelihood of God's existence and correct interpretation of divine commands. To humanists, good reason would suggest that God, if demanding such destruction, is not to be relied upon; good reason suggests belief in such a God is radically mistaken. Yet, as humanists regretfully conclude, when religion is to the fore, good reason loses much power.

Calculative considerations are most famously associated with Pascal and his wager. Pascal argued that belief in God is prudent. Putting up with Sunday or Sabbath confessions is a small price to pay for the possibility, though only the possibility, of eternal and heavenly bliss. Ignoring uncertainties in the calculation, such as which God to worship, how God would assess our initial motivation, and how else belief in God may affect our lives, we simply cannot believe at will or from choice, or, indeed, because we have been threatened. We may decide to go to the synagogue or mosque, but we cannot just decide to believe something – or so it would seem. An ancient challenge making this point is: believe the number of heavenly stars to be even – or odd. Either way, you cannot simply switch on the belief. Regular beliefs need to be responsive to evidence. To believe that something is so is necessarily to believe that it is true that something is so. To be able to believe at will would be akin to magic – as if we could always make something true just by believing it.

As we have seen, humanists reasonably argue that morality is conceptually separate from God and belief in God. Humanists can also make a good case for the 'belief' part of religious belief being rather different from regular belief. Suppose I yearn for Clarissa – and believe that Clarissa secretly loves me. In seeking loving demonstration, I invite her to the opera, ask her round for a drink and send her earrings. My offers are spurned. My conclusion is that opera is not her cup of tea, that she is a non-drinker, and that she lacks desire for earrings. When, the following week, I see her at the opera, having a drink, some splendid earrings jangling – well … ? Maybe, I conclude she plays hard to get. Suppose she resists all my subsequent amatory suggestions. Suppose she sends round her husband, threatens a court order – and eventually calls the police. If I still protest that she loves me really, it is time to recognize that I no longer have a belief, but suffer a forlorn hope, desperate obsession or mental state requiring medication.

Let us now look at some religious matters that suggest some similarity between my 'belief' about Clarissa's love and belief in God. The matters are significant in themselves; hence, the direct discussion and conclusion on religious belief are not reached until this chapter's final section, 'The light of the world'.

The first reason for wondering about religious *belief* is the problem of evil and the religious response. Whatever arcane disputes about ultimate grounds for morality, humanists are struck by the existence of evil, a deadly puzzle for believers in God's love. Believers typically maintain that God is all good – but also all powerful, including all knowing – yet evils, in the form of vast sufferings, exist. Lest we forget, while you read this book, millions of people are suffering malnutrition, natural disasters, disease or war. Think of particular, more homely cases – of toothaches, pains in childbirth, dying and seeing loved ones dying. Add the sufferings of non-human animals. Are not these sufferings gratuitous? Could not God have created a world without them? John Stuart Mill stressed that, looking round the world, we find considerable evidence to blacken any deity's name, not much evidence for praise.

Humanists use reflections such as those above to point to the non-existence of an all-powerful, all-good God. We could argue that we should have sympathy for the Devil or devils; they are overlooked when there is such evidence for their existence, assuming the world is any evidence at all for the supernatural. If the world is evidence for anything supernatural, we arguably should move to the Zoroastrian position – that there exist both good and evil supernatural beings, roughly equal in power. That would be the most rational religious belief – which perhaps explains why there are so few Zoroastrians.

Refinements are required. What counts as 'all powerful' and 'all good'? Could God move an immoveable post? If he is all powerful, he should be able to make such a post; but if all powerful, he should be able to move it. God's omnipotence, though, does not require him to perform the logically impossible. That is no restriction on his power. If told to read this page and not read it at the same time, our inability to obey does not demonstrate poor reading powers. What is logically impossible is, in a sense, nothing at all – so being unable to do the impossible is no failure.

As for being 'all good', some suffering may be good and not gratuitous, for it may be a means towards some consequential benefits, or it may be an unfortunate but inevitable side effect. Suffering the dentist is worth it for the consequent absence of toothache, suffering the hangover for prior pleasurable intoxication. This stance, however, does not readily apply once God is in the frame. A good God apparently holds that certain things are intrinsically bad, and, presumably, prefers goods with no bad side effects than ones with. Perhaps, theists will insist, to reap the rewards of achievements, enduring pains on the way is necessary: achievements require struggle. Maybe the natural laws necessary for human life also necessarily generate disasters such as earthquakes. More generally, perhaps the existence of good logically necessitates that of evils. If this is so, an interesting consequence flows – the Good God paradox. Suppose the presence of goodness necessarily requires some evil. Well, God, we are sometimes told, did not have to create the world. So, now, further suppose that God did not create the world; that is, only God exists. Paradoxically, God could not then be all good – for goodness, it is claimed, requires some evil.

Whatever the power of these considerations, we leave them to one side. Even if some evil is required for the existence of good, that does not account for the vast quantity of worldly suffering, be it the result of human actions that generate moral evils, actions such as murder and torture, or the result of non-human actions, such as floods, earthquakes, pandemics and famine, which generate natural evils.

A well-known attempt at explaining why moral evils are compatible with God's existence is the free will defence. God created human beings with free will, such beings possessing far greater value than programmed robots; but the existence of such free agents entails the possibility of doing evil – and, as it happens, many evils are done. There are deep puzzles about the nature of free will – puzzles for theists and humanists – but the defence's distinctive puzzle is its reliance on God's creating this particular world of free agents rather than another. Assuming God could choose, and also knew what humans would freely choose to do, why did he not create a different world in which humans freely chose to do fewer evils? Further, the defence, of course, lacks credibility in explaining most natural evils, unless – as sometimes claimed – people suffer these natural evils because of their fathers' sins. To humanists this last thought is morally repugnant. What can be morally just about our suffering now because of what great, great, great ... grandfathers did? It merits, I suggest, the quip that, if God exists, it shows his nature in its true light – for he is said to be the ultimate father.

Traditional religious belief is maintained in the face of such evidence against God's goodness. This aids the thought that religious belief is no straightforward belief. It is more like a commitment come what may; more like my belief in Clarissa's love.

A second reason for thinking that religious belief is not just an extremely grand typical belief is brought out in the following.

Consider Sophie and Safia, Sophie brought up Christian and firmly remaining one; Safia brought up Muslim and firmly remaining one. Both recognize that had they been brought up differently – Sophie as Muslim and Safia as Christian – they would have been committed to different religious beliefs. Importantly for this example, these two believers recognize, in a detached way, that evidence for Christianity is of the same strength and character as that for Islam. Knowing that their particular religious belief depends so heavily on their upbringing and culture – and knowing that there is no worldly evidence or tests to show one is right, the other wrong – each would seem to be irrational in holding fast to her belief. Humanists rightly find it utterly irrational that, say, Christians can be so confident in their Christianity when they agree that, had they been brought up a few miles away, across a border, they would be Muslims confident in Islam. All that again should make us wonder quite what is the nature of the belief in religious belief.

It is true that Sophie may describe any experiences she has of God in Christian terms, making reference to the Son and the Holy Spirit, whereas Safia's descriptions may be in different terms, perhaps invoking Mohammed. Yet they both would recognize that, had they grown within the other religion, they would doubtless have been describing their experiences differently. Indeed, personal revelations raise questions of why such experiences or, for that matter, reports of miracles, should be indicative of anything divine at all. We have common ways of checking what people mean by 'mountains', 'money' and 'marmalade' and whether there is a mountain to climb, money to invest or marmalade to spread; but how can it be established whether someone heard the voice of the Holy Spirit or Mohammed – or was merely 'hearing voices'?

The reply may be that such divine experiences are in no worse position than toothaches. No one else experiences this particular toothache of mine – yet it is real and affects my behaviour. The reply to the reply relies on a difference. The ache cannot exist independently of the suffering person, yet the religious experiences are claimed to be of an independent divine being. That makes all the difference – for how can the independence be certified?

Here is a very silly example. The silliness is not to ridicule believers, but for the sake of vivacity. Suppose some people speak of hearing the mysterious voice of a giant supernatural talking turnip, yet no such turnip can be seen, touched or heard by most others. The turnip hearers build up rituals concerning turnips, have turnip talks, develop sacred turnip grounds, with the Holy Turnip Basilica. We have here a religious way of life. We see their rituals, but we should resist thinking their experiences were really of the Holy Turnip, despite the capital 'H' and 'T'. Yes, this is a silly example; but it shows how utterly irrational it is to live a life solely on the basis of voices unheard by many and untestable. Whatever the 'revelations', what the voices claim needs to be assessed. As for reports of miracles, well, reason should typically lead us to think, as Hume recommended, that the reports are more likely inaccurate than that the miracles occurred.

Praise be to God

A woman finds her child alive and well within the volcanic·
ashes, surrounded by many other children who are dead, dying
or maimed. 'Praise God,' she proclaims. The woman is not blind
to the sufferings of others – she is keen to help them – she is,
though, blind to the absurdity of praising God for her child's
safety, but not condemning God for the others' sufferings. For
many believers, however badly things go, godly belief is maintained. Some even boast of believing in defiance of the contrary
evidence. Again, it looks as if religious belief is very different from
beliefs as we usually understand them.

If nothing can possibly count as evidence in the empirical
world against God's existence, do we even possess a proper grip
on what is meant by 'God exists' and what constitutes belief that
God exists? How could we tell we were meeting God, rather
than dreaming? Bradlaugh, encountered in Chapter 1, thought
the concept of God lacked sense. Sympathy for Bradlaugh
increases, when we encounter jumbled tales of the Trinity and
transubstantiation. True, there are jumbled and obscure notions
in quantum physics, but they form part of theories open to predictive evaluation and revision. Mind you, things are not that
straightforward: theories may be clung to, seemingly through
thick and thin. Imre Lakatos illustrates such clinging with a
story of how a scientific theory may be protected, even though
a predicted planet fails to show. Such planetary 'misbehaviour'
is explained away by supplementary hypotheses, pleas for new
research funding and when all these fail – well, the recalcitrant
predictions are consigned to dusty volumes, spoken of no more.
In reality, scientific theories are not dropped just because of a
few instances of counter evidence. None the less, for theories to
have substance, they link somewhere along the line to experience, perhaps through related research programmes and other
testable theories.

What sense can we make of the hypothesis that God exists? Once, particular events were considered evidence for God's existence. Perhaps the just on earth would prosper while rogues would not; praying for rain – to the right God – would bring forth rain; sacrifices for victory in battle would bring victory. Of course, prayers and sacrifices are not remotely reliable – and always a problem when both battling sides pray for success. Furthermore, there is no reason to believe that the just do flourish here on earth. A traditional response, based on the unfounded belief that justice must ultimately prevail, is that such earthly injustice provides a reason to believe in the afterlife when all injustices are ironed out. Apart from the argument's oddness, it raises the question of how to achieve an afterlife. It is unfortunate for millions of non-Christian believers if it must be through belief in Jesus Christ as Son of God. Further, what sense can be made of afterlife experiences? As Charles Dunbar Broad, a twentieth-century Cambridge philosopher, once quipped about such matters, all we can do is: wait and see – or, alternatively, not see.

Stress upon the possibility of verification or falsification as a criterion for statements making sense used to be fashionable; it enabled swift dismissal of metaphysical statements concerning God's existence. Swift dismissal itself was dismissed: how could the underlying verification principles themselves be verified or falsified? Could claims about the past be verified or falsified? By whom and when … ? Although verification–falsification criteria have been resurrected under glossy new labels such as 'anti-realism', there is today a casual readiness to treat the statement 'God exists' as making sense. That is, of course, a far cry from saying that it is true. What could make it true? That is often considered a knock-down question; but it is not. The answer is simple: the existence of God. But further reflection allows us to see that the answer is not simple. This is because God's existence is usually taken to be necessary existence. All the things around us, it seems, might not have existed. You and I might not have existed. This does not appear to apply to God, as earlier seen when discussing Leibniz's cosmological argument about contingencies. God, it is argued, is a necessary existent.

Necessary existence need not be that surprising. The prime number between eighteen and twenty necessarily exists; but if numbers are objects at all, they are abstract objects, lacking causal powers. The number nineteen does not cause anything; yet God, as traditionally understood, is a necessarily existent creator-designer of the world, capable of intervening. So, God continues to be odd – as are the *a priori* arguments for his existence, the ontological arguments. In one simple format, the argument is that God necessarily exists because the concept of God is the concept of something perfect, with maximal reality; and existence is part of maximal reality. Although Bertrand Russell threw his tobacco pouch into the air with delight, when finally thinking the argument sound, he quickly lost conviction. Humanistic thinkers today tend to laugh such arguments out of court, dreaming up examples of perfect pizzas and, indeed, seemingly perfectly sound arguments for both God's existence and non-existence, to show that if any ontological arguments were sound, then these other items would also necessarily exist.

The original ontological argument, from the twelfth-century St Anselm, ran with the thought that God is that being than which nothing greater can be conceived. Now, suppose that he does not exist, then he would not be the greatest conceivable being, for there could be conceived the greater being, namely a God actually existing. But it is contradictory for there to be something greater than the greatest conceivable; hence, our starting supposition that God does not exist is faulty. God does and must exist. Arguably, behind some versions of the argument, there resides a conflation of the idea of X with X. The idea of water is not wet; but what it is an idea of – water – is wet. If God were to exist, then he would be greater than the idea of

God, but not greater than what the idea is an idea of. Indeed, it has been ironically argued that something truly great would be all the greater for being able to do things without even requiring existence.

Most humanists, and, indeed, many believers, judge ontological arguments as mere word play; yet we ought not to be so smug. After all, similar 'word play' has led to fascinating discoveries in mathematics and can lead us to see what cannot exist, for example, a greatest prime number. Perhaps, though, that thought shows a possible mistake in ontological arguments, namely assuming in the first place that we can make sense of the greatest conceivable or most perfect being.

A light on the world

Perhaps our little reflections, on love for Clarissa, on the problem of evil, on Sophie and Safia and on necessary existence, cast religious belief in a new light. Perhaps our reflections suggest religious belief overall is all too much to be typical belief. Rather, religious belief is a way of seeing the world; it too casts things in a different light. To believe that God exists is not to think that there is an item that could be discovered, an item for which there is evidence. To believe that God exists is to treat the world in a certain way.

People who read the world in the light of Christian scriptures see it differently from those who read it in the light of, say, Darwinism and nothing more. Belief in God is part of a web of religious beliefs, the web best understood as expressing commitment to a way of life, be it to help the poor or kill the infidels. On this understanding – and a few religious believers agree – religious claims are expressions of moral intentions, combined with a mixture of exemplary stories, poetry and some empirical claims promoting ways of living. For some Christians, stories of

Jesus' death, the events of the Last Supper and the good Samaritan parable, all lead to living agapeistically – that is, in brotherly love. Richard Braithwaite, a twentieth-century empiricist philosopher, gave explicit voice to the above approach and, on that basis, entered the Church of England. Viewed in this way, religious belief may be seen by some, for example, Marx and Freud, as but a projection of the hopes and fears of humankind; but there is no need to go along with such speculative psychological explanations.

Most believers, of course, take their godly belief to be that there literally exists some supernatural being, that Christ really rose from the dead and that God speaks to them. The proposal that religious beliefs amount only to highly important lifestyle commitments, combined with stories and some regular beliefs, carries with it the thought that traditional theists are mistaken in treating their religious beliefs as involving genuine beliefs about an *existent* necessary being – a little in the way that I am mistaken about my psychological state directed towards Clarissa. A few church and synagogue attenders make no such mistake at all, for they think of themselves as non-believing Christians or Jews, that is, atheists who yet value the tradition, ritual and morality of their religion.

The proposal, then, is that religious belief involves certain commitments and attitudes towards the world – reverence, awe – with the promotion of moral behaviour, sustained by fictions and some historical facts. However gently humanists may suggest this to the religious – perhaps emphasizing the great value of fiction and art for encouraging good living – traditional believers insist that God literally exists. I then reply, 'It's just a way, a valuable way, of seeing the world, leading, say, to encouraging brotherly love, and being in awe of the beauty of sunsets.' They respond, 'But God *really* does exist.' Paradoxically, I may agree – for I may take those words to mean that the speakers really do have the commitments mentioned.

THE GOD-INTOXICATED ATHEIST

Spinoza (1632–1677) was a splendid humanist, yet god-intoxicated. Because of this latter feature, humanists do not readily identify with him. After all, his major work, *Ethics*, talks a lot about God, 'proving' his existence four times over. Yet Spinoza's God does not stand outside the universe, as creator-designer, as a being with purposes and concerns. Spinoza's God is the one totally independent being; God includes the universe (panentheism) or, in a way, they are identical (pantheism) – hence, the atheist tag.

Living in tolerant Holland, Spinoza was not burned at the stake. Yet because of his questioning spirit from early on, at the age of twenty-three he received curses, courtesy of his Amsterdam synagogue, Talmud Torah, in its excommunication of this gentle man.

> Cursed be he by day and cursed be he by night; cursed be he when he lies down and cursed be he when he rises up. Cursed be he when he goes out and cursed be he when he comes in. The Lord will not spare him, but then the anger of the Lord and his jealousy shall smoke against that man, and all the curses that are written in this book shall lie upon him, and the Lord shall blot out his name from under heaven. And the Lord shall separate him unto evil out of all the tribes of Israel, according to all the curses of the covenant that are written in this book of the law.

Spinoza's philosophical writings, sometimes obscure, maybe ultimately muddled, gave rise to pictures of the universe – a dome of many colours – inspiring Shelley, Coleridge, George Eliot and many more. We humans, and, indeed, all creatures and items, are rather like waves on an ocean. To lead the good life, we need to understand our place in nature. Religion is a natural phenomenon to be investigated, the Bible merely a collection of historical documents. Spinoza thus undermined ecclesiastical authority, arguing strongly for free speech, toleration and democracy.

Humanists and Spinoza have much in common, their thoughts separated mainly by language's imagery.

This is where the 'really's multiply. 'But, really, really, really God exists.' 'Yes,' I answer, 'Really, really, really you are committed to loving your fellow humans and being in awe of sunsets …'

The resort to understanding certain basic beliefs as more akin to lifestyle commitments is not unknown. Some suggest that 'the future resembles the past' and 'every event has a cause' are best understood as expectations or rules for investigation – though, in contrast to religion, these we cannot live lives without.

Casting things in different lights, expressing different attitudes, need not thereby be arbitrary, without foundation. It may dovetail with believers' talk of insights and added depths. Life is not 'really' a gift from God, but observations about life as divinely given may encourage respect and pious feeling. Christ represented as crucified in Belsen, talk of Christ remaining within the world – these may bring home humankind's inhumanity and the need to overcome that inhumanity. Odd pictures of the world help us to handle the world. Think of how physicists speak of 'charms', how geneticists lapse into 'selfish' genes, and how chemists picture molecules. It is true that scientific theories lead to tests and experimentation; but the pictures and tales drawn by religions lead to ways of living – some that humanists welcome; some they rightly flee.

Humanists draw pictures. Dawkins pictures human beings as rebelling against genetic tyrants. Liberals picture people breaking free of chains. In Chapter 7, we muse further upon how we find meaning in the world and in our lives by seeing them cast in different lights – lights often shone by art and literature, by metaphor and music, be it religious or not.

4

With morality

Wonders are many, and none is more wonderful than man ...
he has taught himself the arts of speech, of wind-swift thought
and of all the moods for community living and neighbourliness.

Sophocles

Suppose that, at the flip of a switch, you could bring the world's
woes to an end. You could feed the hungry, release the tortured,
and cure the sick. Suppose, too, that the flip would enable people
to laugh and flourish. Your finger draws near; but you suddenly
notice a little girl – and now you realize that, for the switch flip-
ping to work, you must torture this speck of harmless humanity, wrecking her body with unmerited pain. You are to erect
the world's happiness, humanity's joys and all that is good, on
this single girl's unexpiated tears. Would you not clench your
fists, paralysed over what to do? Would you not be filled with
loathing towards whatever power placed you in such a position?
Could you ever be so certain of what is right and wrong that
you would welcome the opportunity – welcome the decision
to flip, or not?

Lest this scenario – derived from Dostoevsky – be dismissed
as so much phantasy, we draw two scenes, far from phantasy,
which raise similar dilemmas, though in lower key.

Three hijackers, mid-flight, take control of a passenger
plane, two hundred holidaymakers aboard. The hijackers' intentions are unclear; radio communication is not at its best. As the
plane circles, the hijackers demand political asylum; yet evidence suggests they could be terrorists, about to crash the plane
in rush-hour London, with thousands of lives lost or maimed.

Should the military shoot down the plane, while it flies over a heath? True, there would be the death of innocent holiday-makers, the hijackers (who may indeed be escaping a repressive regime) and maybe a few people walking their hounds; but the risk of greater tragedy would certainly be avoided.

You are driving home, over alcohol and speed limits – and, let me add, overtired. The steering wheel shudders. You have knocked down a cyclist. You see in your mirror that he is getting up. Probably he is not badly hurt; but he is dragging his leg – maybe broken. You would normally run to help; yet, right now, you want no involvement at all. The police would be called; you would lose your licence. Your ambulance job requires you to drive. Employment is difficult to come by; your husband is unemployed – and you have three children to support. Perhaps the best and right thing to do is to drive on, before your number is taken.

The above raise questions of what we morally ought to do. Let us note: the legal and moral are not identical. It may be perfectly legal to pass by on the other side, when seeing a man in the gutter; but it is usually morally wrong. It may be morally right to demonstrate against a war, yet illegal so to do. In this chapter, we review the resources available to humanists for coping with the moral questions.

Human dignity

Morality concerns what we ought or ought not to do, should or should not do, of good and bad, right and wrong; but that characterization alone fails to attain morality's heart. If you want to shoot someone, you ought to find a gun. If you want to rob, best survey the scene first. Such language, though, does not suggest that these are morally the right things to do. Morality typically demands that we do not shoot or rob, even if we do these things by the best means available. Morality is not a matter of securing the best means for an end that we may just happen to want. Morality involves deciding on the best ends.

Humanists readily speak of morality being grounded in human values and the values in human nature. Humanists are not thinking in terms simply of what humans happen to value, but of values that in some, no doubt obscure, way express humanity. We may wonder, of course, why we should assume that there is one human nature. How similar is male human nature to female? Ignoring that puzzle, it is human nature that has generated centuries of belief in God, gods and divine justifications for killing. So, humanists have to be careful in what they praise about human nature. Indeed, one line of humanism, an existentialist line, has stressed that human nature is as much of a myth as God. What then may we make of the concept of 'human nature'?

The nature of a Euclidean triangle is to have three sides and of adult frogs to have four legs. For a figure to be such a triangle, it *must* have the three, but we know of unfortunate frogs – those born malformed or impinged upon by a cruel world – that lack the four. The lack results from causes interfering with how things would otherwise have biologically developed. It is, we may say, proper to frogs to be quadrupeds, but this implies no commitment to a fixed metaphysical essence of frogs.

Humans are like frogs – well, a little. It is proper to adult humans to have four limbs, even though some do not. Of course, such biological features provide little grounding for a moral sense; but moral sense is both proper to, and distinctive of, humans; limbs are not. A moral sense holds true of humans, even though a few may lack or deny it.

Humans distinctively possess the reflective ability to consider not merely the best means of achieving things, but also what it is best to achieve. This ties in with perceiving ourselves as able and needing to make choices; that is, morality demands a conception of our being free agents. We recognize differences between what is the case and what morally ought to be the case – between what we may want to do and what we morally ought to do. We sometimes act because we ought, not because we want, so to do. Morality imbues many of our beliefs and actions, not merely in terms of good and bad, right and wrong, but in a wealth of evaluative features. Humans admire, resent, feel remorse, experience compassion, become angry, indignant – and much more. Circumstances can justify and make appropriate such emotions and feelings.

Humanism's focus on human dignity is a focus on our sense of morality. It focuses on our being valuers. This requires reflectiveness, enquiry and belief; and the Sophoclean epigraph's reference to wind-swift thought may be viewed in this light.

What of Sophocles' reference to language? Well, to possess concepts, certainly those of morality, we need language; and we need moral concepts to be moral agents, that is, wittingly to do what is right or wrong. Human beings, in contrast to others, can do the right thing *because* it is the right thing – and this involves reflective evaluation. Such evaluative ability does not mean that in all circumstances we should actually reflect and evaluate. Suppose a distressed man is struggling to avoid drowning. Even to pause to wonder whether to help him rather than merely observe, running no risk of muddying new stilettos, already manifests callousness. We ought immediately to help; and, if later asked why, we point to his distress. When an action is likely to generate moral assessment, reflecting on what one ought to do is often part of the right thing to do, but not always – as just shown.

Reflection and valuations are not sufficient to get us to what is morally right and wrong. Many bad things are valued by people, even after reflection. When we learn moral terms we learn that they involve concern for how things go for others and what counts as their going well for others – for neighbourliness and fellow feeling. That learning also involves our becoming concerned for others – the neighbourliness itself. The neighbourly extent has grown and greened over the years – concern, by some, stretches beyond the family, the town, the nation, to all peoples, to animals, to rainforests, the wilderness and seas. Virtually all people recognize the moral significance of others; and most display it to some greater or lesser extent. This concern for others is typical of morality, though not sufficient. The chimp, no doubt, is right in caring for its baby chimps, but it lacks the ability to be caring *because* it appreciates it is right.

Talk of our concern for others is vague talk; but such concern, such involvement with the interests of others, is essential to morality as is the preparedness to let that concern, that involvement, override our immediate wants. We are able to put ourselves in the metaphorical shoes of others; and often we do. We also readily deploy – and, from a young age, deploy – notions of fairness, reciprocity and even the question 'what if everyone did such and such?' Thus, we manifest moral awareness and quickly become aware of dilemmas, such as those opening this chapter. Humanism is right to point out that we possess a variety of moral values – indeed, a motley crew, values often pulling in different directions, rocking us to and fro, as we seek to navigate the good ship life through the storms of life, ours and others.

Morality, understood as involving reflective neighbourliness, leads some to ask: why be moral? Another way of raising that question is to ask humanists: why select those features of humanity – the concern for others, for fairness and so on – to recommend as moral, as what ought to motivate us, rather than other features? After all, human beings, maybe by nature, are often ruthless, selfish and cruel. Whichever features we tie to morality, though – helping others, obeying God or being selfish – someone sceptical, doubtful, may simply ask: why *should* I perform those actions? We may at least rightly say that they morally should do what they morally should do. Even here, nihilists may respond that there is nothing that one ever *should* do; but humanists are in no worse position than theists in answering such sceptics. Sceptics, as noted, could challenge and defy morality even were it grounded in God's commands.

Because of the reference to human nature, humanists are sometimes taken to be relativists or subjectivists. Occasionally they think they are, ending up claiming that moral judgements are mere matters of how we feel or what is useful for us – optimistically relying on the good luck that most of us approve of neighbourliness and so forth. Humanists, though, do not have to meander down that path; and there are some heavy blockages en route. Most tellingly, relativists, were they consistent, would have to accept that relative to some groups' desires or beliefs, authoritarianism – insisting on female genital mutilation, for example – is morally right for those groups. Yet relativists, of a humanist bent, want to say that such intolerance and treatment just is wrong, full stop. Humanists typically are not, then, relativists – and should not be. This is no place to take the matter further.

Those disinclined towards moral scepticism and relativism – indeed, I doubt whether we can live the life of a moral sceptic – and who recognize that God is of no help, often turn to theory. They seek a theory that offers some unified account of what morality is and demands. Humanists can be drawn to such a theory; more accurately and, arguably unhelpfully, though paradoxically also helpfully, humanists offer more than one theory. The theories conflict, but they highlight features that we humans consider of great significance, not least a concern for others, for rational reflection and for things going well.

People are attracted by big theories – by 'isms'. Many seek *the* big theory that offers an all-embracing principle, showing what we morally ought to do – and showing why it is rational to do it or why we should be so motivated. God, we may quip, offers the biggest (attempted) answer; but, with the demise of God, to what may we turn – if turn we need? Some of us believe that any theory runs the risk of distortion, the risk that we distort our moral thinking to fit the theory. If we are going to run that risk, we need very good reasons to do so. Indeed, we may think that there is a similarity between how conscientious religious believers seek to reinterpret texts to salve their conscience and how humanist thinkers reinterpret or modify their favoured big theory to cohere with their existing basic moral beliefs. Let us see how things go with a mainstream approach, namely, utilitarianism, an approach often followed by humanists – and then look at other approaches.

More happiness

Utilitarianism, in the English-speaking world, has in sight the nineteenth-century philosophers, Jeremy Bentham and John Stuart Mill, both associated with humanistic thinking. For such utilitarians 'utility' is associated with happiness – sometimes identified with pleasures; sometimes, satisfactions – or what is conducive to happiness. What determines an action's rightness is the overall consequences, consequences found, of course, in the future. Right actions are those with consequences whereby overall happiness is maximized. When we have a choice, we should select that which maximizes happiness or, if we have a bleak example, minimizes suffering. Your own individual happiness counts in assessing the overall outcome, but it receives no privileged position: utilitarianism is impartial. Optimists – and Mill was one – would hope that many people would secure some happiness simply from helping others.

Utilitarianism manifests some important features of morality. First, it shows that, reflecting about the future, we often wonder what we ought to do as opposed to what we want to do.

Secondly, it manifests our interest in the welfare of others. Thirdly, it brings consistency to our actions by deriving them all from one simple, internally consistent theory; and this latter feature encourages impartiality. All these facets are distinctive of human concerns – arguably, distinctive of human beings at their best. How should that last evaluative comment stand? The immediate answer is: 'in utilitarian terms'; but, paradoxically, utilitarians often realize that the greatest happiness may well be achieved by sticking to simple rules for some cases, and acting spontaneously for others, rather than performing utilitarian calculations. As John Austin, a friend of Mill, pointed out: the lover should not have his eye on the common welfare, when eager to kiss his mistress. Were calculations to occur in such relationships, the relationships would be tarnished; and so – as love is an ingredient of much happiness – happiness would be diminished. We must, then, distinguish between the criterion for what makes an action right and the motive that individuals should have.

Utilitarianism – as with other moral theories – confronts problems of justification. Mill's apparent attempted justification is that because we each desire our own happiness, we morally should aim at the general happiness. Yet, even if people seek their own happiness, how does that show that happiness, and also overall *maximization*, are what should be sought? Most generally, just because something is desired, it does not follow that it is worthy of desire. Even if Mill shows that what I desire is worthy of being desired and, further, that what people, in general, desire is worthy of being desired and if, for that matter, it can be shown that what people desire has much in common (let us say 'happiness'), it still does not follow that *I* should also seek or desire that everyone gets what they desire; indeed, that is probably to desire an impossibility.

Utilitarianism raises further questions. Happiness – what is it? How do we find a common measure of different people's and different types? Such questions fuel those who mock utilitarian's association with the 'dignity of man'. They unwittingly reveal their own low view of humans by assuming that utilitarian happiness must be equivalent to sensual gratifications. Mind you, in Bentham's utilitarianism, poetry and pushpin, if they create the same quantity of pleasure, do possess the same value – pushpin being a child's game, though some have suggested a sexual reading. Crude Benthamite hedonism, though, is no part of the humanist stance and need be no part of utilitarianism. Mill argued that poetry generates higher pleasures than pushpin – in either reading, I suspect. Once people experience a range of pleasures, some are often recognized as more valuable than others. People even agree over many of the some. True happiness perhaps is recognized as consisting in a flourishing life, a life that involves far more than satisfying basic desires for immediate pleasures.

We need to say more about consequences and maximization. Ignoring difficulties of assessing probabilities, do we seriously think that what makes an action right hangs on overall consequences, including, therefore, those of many generations later? Consider this: because a sixteenth-century woman had a child, many generations later Hitler was born. Had that woman not borne the child, Hitler would not have come into being and hence, perhaps, there would have been no Holocaust. Maybe the overall outcome for the world would have been better had that woman been murdered when a child. Of course, the woman did not intend to be a remote cause of Hitler's existence; the actions she performed were, say, those of a loving lover and then mother.

Utilitarianism can scramble out of blaming the woman. As we saw with Austin's kiss example, happiness maximization being the desirable state does not necessarily make it the best motive to have. The motives and character of our sixteenth-century woman may be applauded, even though, in this instance, they eventually led to something exceptionally bad. A powerful criticism of utilitarianism, though, still stands, namely that the doctrine runs the risk of encouraging us to treat people merely as a means to an end – the end of happiness.

Suppose it necessary to torture someone in order to secure certain benefits. Is morality merely interested in whether the proposed torture maximizes benefits compared with other possible actions? Most of us have a feeling that some considerations trump – outweigh – such calculations. Suppose a healthy person could be killed, his organs distributed, to save the lives of many others in need of organ transplants. On crude utilitarian reasoning, killing the healthy person would seem the right thing, if the benefits outweigh other factors, for example, the unhappiness caused by general insecurity, were the policy known. Yet, considerations, other than beneficial consequences, should surely come into play. We readily fall into talk of human rights. Whatever the outcome, it seems obviously wrong to kill someone for their organs against their will. 'Surely, I have a right to my body for myself, come what may.'

'Rights' talk gave rise to a splendid jibe from Bentham: it is nonsense on stilts. He was thinking of natural rights, of there being something about nature or about God that determines these rights independently of everything else. Utilitarianism has room for rights, but only those created by us, justified through aiding maximizing happiness. Perhaps overall happiness is promoted, only if there is the stability that results from having rights to property, our body, a fair trial and so on. It is the overall happiness that 'wears the trousers'.

Turning to this chapter's opening dilemmas, utilitarianism recognizes no deep dilemmas, just practical problems of prediction from an impartial viewpoint. In opposition is the thought that there just are some morally important partialities.

Suppose you can save only one person, either your child or an unknown individual. Ought you to calculate the different possible happiness outcomes in order to decide whom to save? Would not morality demand that you save your child because she is your child? Utilitarians may reply that saving one's own child maximizes happiness because it helps to develop flourishing relationships. However, to justify your saving your child by such a thought would be 'one thought too many'. Although, as we saw with the lover's kiss, utilitarians need not be saddled with recommending utilitarianism as people's typical motivation, they remain open to the charge that they sometimes misunderstand what makes an action the right action. Saving your own child is not right *because* it helps to maximize overall happiness. Maybe it is the right thing to do, full stop.

Utilitarianism also raises problems of fairness and distribution. The drowning child example points to the importance of certain partialities which utilitarianism needs to accommodate within its

'THE END HAD CEASED TO CHARM'

Humanists are not necessarily optimistic about human beings, though many feel that some human progress can be made, by way of improving people's lives – and some progress undoubtedly has been made. Slavery, in general, is no longer tolerated; welfare has been improved in some (lucky) parts of the world.

One optimistic humanist was John Stuart Mill (1806–1873), the highly influential utilitarian of the nineteenth century, who encouraged education and improved welfare conditions – so that people may have the opportunity to realize their potential.

Mill was something of a genius, learning Latin and Greek while still a child. Unsurprisingly, he had a nervous breakdown, reflecting that even if everything for which he fought were to come about, he would still feel empty; 'the end had ceased to charm'. The poetry of Wordsworth and Coleridge helped him out of this – as did the love of a good woman, Harriet Taylor. What a pity that she was already married ...

impartiality; yet there are further problems with its particular application of impartiality. A society may secure overall maximum happiness, if some people are victimized, badly treated, perhaps enslaved. If A happens to get more pleasure out of something than B, then should not A deserve preference – if we seek overall happiness? Suppose, on the one hand, a phantasy in which a few people, gluttons, possess a huge capacity for happiness, far exceeding that of all others combined: it would seem resources should go to the gluttons rather than others. Utilitarianism fails to give easy voice to the idea of fair distributions between individuals. Suppose, on the other hand, we would maximize happiness by having large swathes of people each with only a teeny amount of happiness, rather than a much smaller population with considerable happiness each. Crude utilitarianism is trapped with the former option; its impartiality is applied to units of happiness rather than individual people. This raises the question of whether happiness maximization is more likely to be achieved by creating more people or by improving the lot of existing people. Should we make more happy people or make (existing) people more happy?

These puzzles involving rights, partiality, flourishing lives, fairness, have to be handled by any moral theory. Utilitarianism has various shaky detailed responses; it also has an easy general response. The easy general response is that once happiness maximization is properly understood, we shall see that it requires some degree of fairness in distribution, an appreciation of partialities as part of the flourishing life – and so on. That is very easy to say, not so easy to work out.

More than happiness

Let us note what is happening above. A theory is meeting our pre-existing moral judgements, rather than the other way round. It is not always a one-way route. There is a two-way interaction, but no easy answers in the way that people often want, of simply establishing the key theory, independently of our particular moral judgements. Utilitarianism concentrates on human flourishing, on welfare. It then has difficulty in two areas: impartial rights and the partiality of personal relationships. So, utilitarianism is revised to account for these added elements of our moral interests. Does this suggest that such a moral theory has no value, being at the mercy of our pre-existing moral prejudices? Not at all; it is part of our reflective behaviour, helping us to see our actions cast in new lights, showing consistencies and inconsistencies, and maybe changing what we think we ought to do. Any proposed theory, though, has no last word. Our moral judgement in particular cases has the first word, and – after the toing and froing between particular judgements and general principles – if a last word is needed, it is usually our judgement in a particular case.

Let us view other approaches, to pick up some of the elements in our motley morality that generate difficulties for utilitarianism. One element is the impartiality expressed in terms of rights; the other is the moral relevance of partialities. We turn to the partialities later in this chapter; but first, we examine the impartial 'rights' approach, an approach that views consequences as forming the wrong starting point. Rightness, it is argued, is not determined by outcomes. Kant is the key figure here; we met him in Chapter 1, as the hugely influential Enlightenment philosopher. For Kant, as for utilitarians, humanity grounds morality, but for Kant this has nothing directly to do with happiness. The Kantian search is for principles, authorized by reason, which are consistently applicable to all human agents. Through reason, we can see that there are some duties we must respect, irrespective of actual consequences. Theories that understand morality in terms of such duties are deontological.

If you morally *ought* to do something, then it must surely be something that you *can* do: 'ought' implies 'can' – well, so it seems. It cannot be morally incumbent upon me to stop the tsunami, if I lack preventive power. This provides the idea that morality demands that we are free – or at least that we view ourselves as free. What is it to be free? It is to obey ourselves, that is, to be autonomous; but, according to Kant, we are not autonomous, when driven by passions and desires. We are truly obeying ourselves only when acting from our rationality. To follow desires, lusts, appetites, is to be caused, showing ourselves as slaves or as trees rocked by storms. Morality bites when we are free agents, originators of what we do, thus making our actions truly ours. 'Autonomy' is the key concept. The autonomous agent must be able to overcome the external demands of desires. He does this when moved by rationality, by what, paradoxically, rationality dictates.

Autonomy leads to Kant's categorical imperative. Hypothetical imperatives depend on the end in view. Even if we all want happiness, deciding what to do on that basis is still hypothetical: ' *given* we want the happiness end, on that hypothesis, this is what we must do.' Categorical imperatives lack the conditional 'if'; they cannot depend on what we happen to want or on accidental circumstances. If my wants and individual circumstances are to be ignored, what is left? The answer is: a point of view, a perspective, removed from my own attached peculiarities; so, it coincides with all other rational agents' points of view, their own peculiarities also deleted. This is a truly impartial viewpoint – and we are familiar with such impartiality when we consider mathematics. That right-angled triangles satisfy certain theorems is true, independently of our peculiar position when thinking about them.

The fundamental categorical imperative, which results from the impartial, the detached, viewpoint, is presented in different versions. We may doubt whether they amount to the same. The

Formula of Universal Law version is 'Act only on that maxim through which you can at the same time will that it should become a universal law.' This maxim is both a test for moral laws and also a motive to action.

Falsely promising is the best example of an action that offends the categorical imperative. Could you will that people falsely promise whenever it suits them? Were that to be the universal law, promising would break down, for promising as an institution requires that people typically do not break promises just when it suits them. Hence, it would be impossible to make any sort of promise; it would be impossible to be motivated to promise truly or falsely, for the institution of promising could not then exist. There would be a contradiction of sorts involved in the willing. Consequently, 'always keep promises' is one manifestation of the categorical imperative.

It is doubtful whether even this best case example works. Why assume that everyone would know about the falsity in promising? And why does the claimed contradiction count for so much? We cannot universalize, 'I will sell hats, but not buy any.' There is a contradiction in everyone selling hats and no one buying any hats; yet selling hats by those who do not buy hats is surely not immoral – so what additional test is required to identify moral duties? Further, Kant's other examples of duty – duties to help others in need, to develop one's talents, not to commit suicide – are difficult to extract convincingly from the test. At best, we may claim that there is something irrational in not following the proposed maxims. Maybe it would be irrational to commit suicide, for my autonomy would be undermining its future. Kant's examples take us somehow, according to Kant, to deriving duties even to refrain from mockery, from self-deceit and drunkenness.

As ever with moral duties, there are questions of motivation and justification. Kant believes reasoning about our moral duties has its own motivating power; so even if we do not do what moral duty demands, we still recognize the demand.

Kant's stress on autonomous agents offers an easier version of the categorical imperative than the one already considered. The easier version is the Formula of the End in Itself: we should treat humanity never simply as a means, but always at the same time as an end. That is, we should respect human beings as individuals, with their capacities to reflect and act – indeed, as autonomous moral agents. Obviously, many of us are used as means – but not solely as means. We are free agents who have voluntarily, well, voluntarily in theory, taken up our occupations; and that is how we morally should be treated. We fail to respect others if, for example, we falsely promise them things. We need to treat others so that they are able to act morally. This approach, focusing on autonomy, gives rise to the idea of individuals possessing rights. We fail to treat others as autonomous agents if we manipulate them, use them for our ends, prevent them from access to the truth, or deny their responsibility, their own moral agency.

Apart from questioning which moral duties result from the categorical imperative however understood, there will be many occasions when, in application, they conflict. Kant tends to be silent about how to prioritize duties, and silent over what to do when even one duty generates conflict. Morally, I should help A; morally, I should help B: yet to help A, I must upset B; and to help B, I must upset A. One Kantian example has Kant insisting that you should not lie to a killer about the whereabouts of his intended victim. You should always tell the truth. Some, though, do argue that there is scope in Kant to allow for exceptions in application.

This is no place for detailed assessment. We merely are showing how a theory, humanistically inspired, is generated – and may then need revision. We should surely lie to the killer to save the victim. We should surely break our promise to be at the party, if suddenly needing to help someone in distress. And just as utilitarianism may be criticized for thrusting theory into our moral agency, so too may deontology. Just as utilitarianism places too much stress on consequences so Kant places too much on respecting the individual agent. Witness his likely response to the first dilemma at the start of this chapter; the response would simply be that one should not torture. Now, that may well be the right response; but is it as quick as that? Is there not a genuine dilemma?

Kant's emphasis, where morality is concerned, is on duty rather than desire; motive rather than outcome; reason rather than cause; action rather than passion, esteem rather than affection. To provide a flavour, consider this from Kant on the good will, the good intention of an individual who fails to achieve an outcome that we recognize as morally valuable:

> Even if it should happen that, by a particularly unfortunate fate
> or by the niggardly provision of a step-motherly nature, this will
> should be wholly lacking in power to accomplish its purpose ...
> and if there remained only the good will (not as a mere wish
> but as the summoning of all the means in our power), it would
> sparkle like a jewel in its own right, as something that had its full
> worth in itself. Usefulness or fruitlessness can neither diminish
> nor augment this worth.

Action, to be morally valuable for Kant, needs to be from duty, not merely in accord with duty. The woman who empties her pockets, giving money to help beggars, is not acting with moral worth, if she does it because she is moved by sympathy; her will is tarnished by natural desire. The man who empties his pocket, with no feeling for the beggar at all – maybe he suffers from the niggardly provision of a step-motherly nature – but because it is his duty ... well, his will sparkles like a jewel. Kant's single-mindedness on impartial respect for individuals has him denying not merely the significance of consequences, but also the significance of possessing the right emotions. Surely, emotions can have a moral significance, a significance, indeed, that fits well with humanism's focus on humanity.

As we have seen, some humanists stress utilitarianism, morality being grounded in our human concern for happiness. Other humanists are more Kantian inspired, grounding morality in our human interest in reason and autonomy. The existence of moral factors other than happiness and autonomy, though, leads many humanists to recognize that such theories require modification and supplementation. Hence, we turn to another humanistic approach to morality – sometimes presented as a theory: virtue theory. As it orientates our moral thinking to the sort of individuals that we should be, rather than principles to follow, it is better labelled: virtue ethics.

Virtue ethics – or Aristotelianism – identifies right actions as those that a virtuous agent would do, when acting in character. We know what the traditional virtues are – such as courage, moderation, justice – but virtue ethics identifies the virtues as those character traits that contribute to eudaimonia. 'Eudaimonia' is often understood as 'flourishing'. Morality bites because of its contribution to our flourishing. We all want to flourish. What is the best way, though without guarantee, of achieving this? Well, acquire habits of courage, moderation, justice – truthfulness, benevolence – rather than follow a theory's principles.

Aristotle's model is that of function. Humanists deny that humans have a function, in the sense of being designed, just as they deny that eyes are designed; but we can recognize that there is something that eyes are best at, something that is proper to them. This thought, it is suggested, may be applied to human beings. It is, of course, questionable what humans are best at – perhaps they are best at deceit, irrationality and jealousy? – but we may at least recognize that typically they are more likely to flourish in some ways rather than others. Most of us value – to varying degrees – truthfulness, compassion, loyalty, courage and generosity. Part of human flourishing is to have friends, to help people out, to be helped out, to stand up for what we believe in – and so on. We may be impressed by the ingenuity and entrepreneurship of some successful business people, but if we learn that their success resulted from metaphorically knifing colleagues, ignoring their children, or letting down their friends, then it is unlikely that they would receive our admiration.

In contrast to Kantian deontology, virtue ethics holds that morally decent human beings should sometimes act from sympathy. You rush to help those who stumble, not from duty but because they are fellow humans. Of course, being virtuous does not require right feelings alone, but also in the right proportion and with the right beliefs. Perfectly compassionate individuals, keen to help others, may think of asylum seekers as not truly human, and so denigrate them or worse. Once the false belief is exposed, their attitudes should change. The question to ask, when uncertain about an action's morality is: would a wise and virtuous person perform the action? We may know whom to ask and we may grasp the answer, even though lacking wisdom and virtue ourselves.

There are obvious criticisms of the approach outlined. Why should we assume that flourishing is the same for all? Further, the ethic seems to give us a rag-bag of moral concerns; but, we may reflect, that is how it should be – for morality is a rag-bag. One problem, though, is what is included in the bag. Aristotle's 'flourishing' included owning slaves and treating women as inferior. Many see humility as part and parcel of the good life, but it is not an obvious virtue for others – certainly not for Aristotle. Although he sees boastfulness as a vice, he is pretty keen on pride. Here, problems of application arise. Quite what, for example, counts as the right extent regarding pride? What is acting courageously? It should not lapse into foolhardiness, yet also not be so watered down that it becomes cowardice.

Problems of application apply to all three aforementioned approaches, even within the terms of each one; but we also need to go outside each one. The Kantian promotion of respect needs tempering by the recognition that consequences are sometimes morally relevant. Utilitarians need to give special weight to rights. Aristotelians should sometimes be worried about overall welfare. And so on. There is a medley of competing moral considerations. The approaches tuck the problems away under different portions of the carpet – yes, a carpet again – be it the brightly single-coloured section of utilitarian happiness, the threadbare yet unyielding section of Kantian duty or the motley patterning of Aristotelian virtues.

Objectivity and dilemmas

Our sketch of various central moral matters brings out: first, humanism's concern for welfare, for reason and rights, for feelings and character; secondly, how moral theories are available without dependence on divinity; thirdly, how there are puzzles within each of the theories; and fourthly, how morality presents a motley array of competing considerations, frequently with no obvious common measuring device. A simple moral theory gives priority (say) to happiness, satisfying our recognition of its moral significance, but, in doing so, the problematical dust of the importance of rights is swept elsewhere. Clean up our thinking on rights and we find we now have trouble with the importance of happiness. Of course, theories may be constructed as eclectic mixtures of moral considerations, weightings being given more to some than others. However, we may then be creating Ptolemaic epicycles, with increasing numbers of ad hoc principles, to recognize pre-existing moral intuitions and improving moral insights.

The toing and froing between general principles revised in the light of our individual moral judgements about particular cases, with those judgements revised in the light of persuasive general principles, could conceivably converge to a reflective equilibrium; but it is wildly optimistic to think that any such equilibrium will ensue, producing answers on *all* moral matters, answers recognized as correct by rational thinkers.

However much people differ, most do though agree on quite a lot about what we morally ought to do. That is hardly surprising. To be part of human society requires language and language requires cooperation. If you do your own thing semantically, it is doubtful whether you can mean anything at all; and certainly you would fail to communicate verbally with others. Lewis Carroll's Humpty Dumpty may seem to make words mean whatever he wants them to mean, but, in explaining this to Alice, he had to use words with their common meaning. And for words to secure a common meaning, humans need some agreement in what they judge to be so. It would be odd, therefore, to think that people could speak a common language of morality without any agreement on what moral terms mean and to what they often apply; but that does not entail always agreeing with others or indeed with our own past judgements – witness this chapter's opening dilemmas.

Some moral conflicts arise from disagreement about the facts – about afterlives, whether capital punishment deters, the likelihood of hijackers being terrorists and the relevance of holy books. Further, even when there are some very general underlying common moral principles, local circumstances may generate moral variations. Concern for people's welfare, in some climates, may mean prohibition on certain foods, prohibitions lifted to moral status. The availability of contraceptives, or property inheritance, may account for differences in sexual moralities. By simple analogy, there is a single mathematical concept of cubing, but if applied to 'local circumstances' of even numbers, outcomes are numerically even; but applied to 'local circumstances' of odd numbers, outcomes are odd. Other moral differences may occur because actions are cast in different lights. Yet, even when we have taken all such factors into account, dilemmas still arise: we discuss some in Chapter 6.

People are often irritated by moral dilemmas, thinking that there must always be 'the' right answer telling them which particular action must be performed. Now, the world of how things are cannot be contradictory; but maybe the moral world of what is right and wrong can be contradictory. It cannot be true that I both did and did not shoot down the plane; but perhaps A could be right in concluding that *he* morally ought to shoot and B, with the same moral considerations and circumstances, could be right in concluding that *he*, B, morally ought not to shoot. Some philosophers, wary of such seeming contradictions, insist that such cases cannot arise, if proper moral weight is granted to all factors – unless the moral weights of the alternatives balance, in which case either action would be morally permissible. Yet often the moral factors, in particular circumstances, seem impossible to compare.

How do we weigh up funding those women who want children and need IVF treatment against using such funds to relieve suffering of the elderly – or enhancing provision of the arts? How do I measure the value of my exercising the right to free speech against not offending some religious friends? In such cases, we still have to act; and, in acting, we help make ourselves who we morally are. Thus it is that we create our moral selves; thus it is that we are self-creating creatures.

In the same circumstances, people may reach opposing decisions, and yet may look back, embracing the different decisions as the right choices. And, I controversially suggest, they could be right so to do. It is in this way that we make who we are. It is in this way that we may display our human dignity.

5

With politics

Two cheers for Democracy: one because it admits variety and two because it permits criticism.

E. M. Forster

How should society be run? Politics raises this question and, on this question, humanists are angels – metaphorical angels, of course.

We humanists do not burn books, take offence at cartoons or threaten prophets who foretell of our eternal torment in hell. We neither persecute people for their beliefs nor repress consensual sex nor insist that women be veiled in public. We issue neither death threats to challengers of humanism nor curses to those who trade in alternative religions, astral experiences or virtual realities. Considerable asymmetry exists between those with faith and us without. Those filled with faith often seek to enforce their way of life on others; we do not. We support a neutral state, a secular state – one which permits people of religion, and those of none, to live lives as they will, so long as harming no others.

Yet, are things so simple? Consider an alternative characterization.

Humanists support laws that, through legitimising abortion and euthanasia, permit the killing of what is most precious to us all, namely, innocent lives – millions of them. Not only that, but humanists permit – even encourage – mockery of our deepest beliefs. Through opposition to faith schools, they seek to impose their atheism on our children, yet our moral and religious duty is to nurture our offspring and community in the uncorrupted ways of God. The so-called neutral state compels us to live confined private lives: we are often banned from displaying religious allegiance, forced to shield ourselves from those around us, who are permitted indecency in dress, in speech and in sexual activity – all works of the Devil.

Our humanist speaks as a liberal – with a small 'l'. Humanists do not have to be liberals – and there are varying degrees and understandings of liberalism – but they usually are liberally inclined. They usually find attractive at least one key element of the United States Bill of Rights, namely, its upholding of the freedom of speech. Humanist associations across the world declare belief in individual freedoms and rights, stressing the importance of individual responsibility, social cooperation and mutual respect. Often, arguably somewhat optimistically, humanists tend to believe that people can and will continue to find solutions to the world's problems, improving the quality of life. Yet the religious, from the fanatic to the lukewarm, demand their rights and freedoms. They too are concerned with life's quality – a life, in their view, probably being eternal, and hence somewhat longer than humanists anticipate. For a few religious believers, laws should be totally determined by scripture; the political becomes little more than scriptural interpretation. How can humanism – humanism, keen on political debate and diversity – respond?

At heart is the puzzle of how those content to tolerate diversity can tolerate the intolerant. Lest readers become optimistic, allow me to say right now that my answer is simple: we muddle through. This chapter displays important features of humanism's liberalism and attempted accommodation of the religious. It is worth adding that humanistic belief in mutual respect may mislead. Writing as humanist, I respect – in the sense of 'admire'

– neither believers nor belief, when the belief is that the right thing is to murder those offensive to religion. However, I respect – that is, acknowledge – believers' autonomy, and tolerate them and the expression of their views.

Conductor or ringmaster?

Consider an orchestra playing a symphony, with, of course, a conductor conducting. The musicians each have their parts; but what they play – the notes, the tempo – is not determined by them. They are no mere cogs in the orchestral machine – they bring individual colour, tone and vitality – but they are not far off cog-like states, being regimented by musical score, conductor's baton and other players' playing. True, they are not thereby playing the same instruments, the same notes and rhythms; they are not as regimented as those in a regiment marching as one.

Consider, now, a circus ringmaster or even traffic police. They impose a certain order, to avoid clashes and crashes, be they between acts or vehicles, but, those apart, the individual actors and drivers are free to act and drive as they choose. The ringmaster does not instruct the lion tamers, clowns – the lovely ladies on the trapeze – what to do in their acts; traffic police neither fix drivers' destinations nor (usually) the routes to be taken.

Primary assessments of orchestral performances are of how well the orchestra performed; individual performances may go unnoticed save as parts of the whole – and when they are assessed, the assessments may, in part, be of their contributions to the whole. All the more so is this with regimental members marching in step; it is but wit when a single marcher insists that he alone was in step. In contrast, circus acts are evaluated individually; the clownish success is unrelated to the tamings of the lion tamer. Of course, there are cases and cases, degrees and degrees.

Should the state, the laws, the government, be more like conductor – or more ringmaster? Should citizens follow life's scores set by law, their lives going well depending on how most others go too? Or should law provide merely the framework, with individuals acting out lives as they think best, maybe largely independent of others? Is our primary aim the flourishing of the community – or of individuals?

Humanism tends towards the ringmaster. Many religious believers – and some others – tend towards the conductor, the musical score often played to God's glory. The hymn 'All Things Bright and Beautiful' usually now, though, does not include

STINGING GADFLIES

From Socrates in ancient Athens to Salman Rushdie in London, some thinkers have dared to sting societies by their thinking – sometimes societies' thanks have been by way of death threats and death. Stinging gadflies are not thereby humanists, but humanists tend to value their desire to speak out and challenge authority.

Socrates was found guilty of heresy and of corrupting the youth. He asked questions about the gods, about political leaders, morality and common beliefs; he meddled. Socrates was urged to flee prison and his death sentence, but stayed firm to his respect for the law. He drank the hemlock.

Galileo, in seventeenth-century Italy, argued merely that Earth orbited the sun; he ended up recanting – not unreasonably so, given the torture on offer. Many tortures and deaths have resulted from people speaking out, seeking to secure social progress – or simply keen to express their thoughts or the truth. Recall the threats – of injury and killings – following the publication of cartoons of Mohammed and Allah. Recall the fatwa against Rushdie, when he had written a work of mere fiction.

As Rushdie noted, 'It is very, very easy not to be offended by a book. You just have to shut it.'

the lines 'The rich man in his castle/The poor man at his gate/ God made them, high or lowly/And order'd their estate.' No longer is there the Christian belief that people were each born to a certain station: contrast with the continuing Hindu caste system.

Religious scores tell people how best to live. Those who favour a completely religious state, say, an Islamic one, would have – shuffling the metaphor – citizens singing from the same hymn sheet imposed by God's will, as stately understood. Many, more realistic, religious believers, lacking confidence in any state upholding their own religious values, prefer a state more secular, not ostensibly tied to religion. Such believers often still seek favourable treatment for their religion; they may still believe that there is but one right basic way to live for all. States may, of course, be religious to greater or lesser extents.

A religious state justifies some laws on the basis of God and scripture. Islamic states turn to the Qur'an for a lot; enfeebled Christian states may have little of Christianity remaining, save through ritual, institutions or certain privileges. The Church of England, for example, remains the established religion in Britain. Once religion is built into law, discrimination may occur against the non-religious and other religions: many people may not want to observe the Sabbath; non-Christians may object to bishops having parliamentary voting rights, and Christian women may be indignant at needing to be considerably covered, if under sharia law.

People differ in desires, aspirations and what makes their lives meaningful. Fortunately, many of those desires, aspirations and values do not conflict. Chess-players who value playing chess are happy so long as allowed to play their chess; they object not at all to others who dislike chess, preferring football instead. There is a plurality of ways of living, good and bad, some involving ways of the sacred, different ways of the sacred, some not. What should the state, its laws, the government do?

The obvious answer is 'live and let live' – the ringmaster answer. Although humanists may present certain lifestyles as superior to others, there is not *one* definitive 'best way' that should be imposed. Humanists recognize that humans form a motley crew; and motley crew they should remain. They recognize too the importance, to many, of religion. People's desires and aspirations, though, sometimes conflict; hence, the ringmaster state sets boundaries, preventing people infringing the freedom of others. This is the 'let live' element of 'live and let live'. It recognizes a pluralism, a plurality of ways to live well.

The neutral state, the secular state, advocated by humanists, is not an atheist state. It neither holds to, nor imposes, atheism. The neutral state could be one in which most individuals, theoretically all, are highly religious, even of the same brand. The value in the state, even in those circumstances, being neutral would be the recognition that others *could* live within that state – perhaps future generations who cast off parents' faith, perhaps immigrants – without being dominated by any state-supported religious laws.

The neutral state accords with traditional humanist emphasis on human beings' dignity, on people who, as valuers of life, should be free to choose how to live. This respects individuals' rights to make choices, though does not thereby respect the choices made. Why such a high priority should be given to the freedom of choice-making is, of course, open to question; but, allowing people to choose is at least one requirement, it is often claimed, for our uncovering what is valuable for life.

This brings us to John Stuart Mill's Liberty Principle, also known as the 'Harm Principle', with 'liberty' and 'freedom' being used interchangeably. Mill announces, 'The only purpose for which power can be rightfully exercised over any member of a civilized community, against his will, is to prevent harm to others. His own good, either physical or moral, is not a sufficient warrant.' Even if harms will occur, promotion of overall welfare may justify no restrictions on the harmful sources: competition between businesses secures benefits for many, yet sufferings result when businesses go out of business. The Mill business goes on; and Mill goes on to say that individuals cannot rightfully be compelled to do something because it will be better for them. We may try persuading them or reasoning with them, but that is all. Individuals are sovereign – with the exception of the insane, children and others in no position to make informed choices. Were you destitute, ravaged by famine, war or disease, it would be wise to settle for regimentation, if it secured food, peace and medical supplies.

Mill's principle applies when informed effective choices are possible. Despite some critical carping, the principle coheres with, and is grounded in, his utilitarianism. A necessary ingredient for flourishing lives is people making their own free choices. People need to be autonomous. To be told what to do – and programmed by state or scripture's blueprint – is to be merely robotic. Some may value robotic lives, but most people value reaching decisions themselves, making their own choices, as how best to live. (For types of liberty, please see Chapter 8's text box.)

The Liberty Principle has often been seen as solely aimed at providing individuals with options; but Mill stresses the need for self-improvement and for human development in its richest diversity. This once again tells us that Mill is keen that individuals should flourish in their own way; this newly tells us that Mill values diversity, maybe believing that societies of diversity are more likely to have individuals faring well than ones of conformity. Humanists tend to agree.

The Liberty Principle speaks of harm; but whatever counts as harm? Presumably stabbing someone with a knife does, but – apparently – offending him does not. Arguing against people is permitted; yet should it be permitted, if it causes tearful responses, making them suffer from shame or loss of friends? There is also the problem of what counts as affecting people, or as *directly* affecting people. The lonely who drink themselves to death are engaged in actions that have nothing to do with others; but if they call on health resources and disgust the neighbours – well, do their actions really lack direct effect on others? Those who install alarms do so to protect their property, yet the alarms invariably cause nuisance to innocent neighbours, though, arguably, rarely to burglars. Are they directly harming the neighbours? Indirectly? Or should such disruptions count as no harm at all?

Line drawing, throughout many walks of life, raises problems. No one in everyday contexts confidently draws the line between the colours red and orange, yet we still can spot clear cases of these colours. The dangers from driving in towns may suggest speed limits around thirty miles per hour; but there is no reason for choosing thirty rather than twenty-nine or thirty point three. We muddle through – and that is how to handle the Liberty Principle. Some yearn for a definition of 'harm'. In response, we should reflect that some indeterminacy would necessarily remain, if the definition is correct. How much an individual's action may affect others comes in degrees, as does how much the effects matter.

We have to do what is reasonable, and that varies from context to context. Mill vigorously defends free speech, yet if the speech, outside a corn-dealer's house, harangues a mob, encouraging it to torch the place, then it is incitement and merits prohibition. 'Incitement', though, also lacks sharp boundaries. Contemporary examples of grey areas abound. What counts as racism, sexism, indeed as restrictions on liberty? Consider recent battles in Britain over fox-hunting, and in the United States over the treatment of suspected terrorists. Consider arguments about discrimination on the basis of sexual orientation, bans on smoking, mobs outside paedophiles' homes (well, sometimes, as a tribute to educational systems, paediatricians' homes) – and so on.

'Live and let live' is not easy to apply; but most people do at least hold the same underlying values – on not harming others, on minorities not being repressed by majorities, on the value of liberty. The disagreements are often disagreements over application. It is when deeply held specific beliefs come into play – beliefs that others lack – that muddling through is not so easy. Christians and atheists want Jack to be a happy Jack, but for Christians that involves eternal afterlife, for atheists, not. Eternal afterlife makes a big difference in calculations about what should be allowed.

Neutrality

Mill's approach justifies the neutral state. The neutral state, being neither atheistic nor theistic, holds the ring between different competing religions and non-religions, between different and competing beliefs. The neutral state, though, cannot be completely neutral. First, in holding the ring, it determines the ring; it needs to impose minimal restrictions to ensure people do not harm others. These restrictions are, we may say, procedural: they are impartial, concerning the public world of voting, applying for jobs, access to shops. Secondly, in having that sort of ring at all, the neutral state is giving autonomous flourishing a very high priority, subject to the procedures set. Thirdly, that is all: apart from the autonomous flourishing and the ring, the neutral state has little more to say, though that 'little more' may grow, the more that welfare needs are recognized as essential to autonomy. Some, though, insist that flourishing lives also require a deeper sense of 'community', a commitment to traditions and additional values. Neutrality hence can come under attack from both the religious and non-religious. Neutrality is seen sometimes as being too light on the values it espouses, sometimes as too heavy with autonomy.

Values pull in different directions. The value of freedom sometimes conflicts with the value of preserving life and that sometimes conflicts with toleration of religious practices. Further, there is no reason to believe that people of different faiths, or of no faith, will agree which value in society should take highest priority, even assuming the same values are recognized. True, we may optimistically propose that the neutral state's concern for individuals' autonomy, for freedom to flourish, is one typically recognized by religious believers. After all, they are usually interested in personal survival after death, in securing converts before death (apparently, after death is too late) and in believers sincerely assenting to God's voice. Maybe these factors suggest that, typically, autonomy secures at least a very high value even for theists. Sincerely to assent to God's voice surely involves freely so doing rather than being coerced. As touched upon earlier, arguably a coerced belief is not truly a belief.

Our use of 'freedom' and 'autonomy' above has been somewhat slippery. Yes, religious authorities seek sincerity in their believers, but they may not support their believers being exposed to, as they see them, false and immoral ways. Those with alcoholic tendencies, valuing a temperate life, may sensibly prefer not to encounter intoxicating temptations. The gullible may value a state that prohibits the silver tongues. The puritanical may need siren voices well silenced. For belief to be genuine belief, faith to be genuine faith, people do not need to hold their belief or faith steadfast in the face of anything, just anything. Paradoxically, steadfastness can provide a criticism of belief: recall Chapter 3's Clarissa. For belief to be genuine belief, faith to be genuine faith, there is no requirement for a neutral blank beginning or clean slate, an impossible requirement indeed. Religious authorities may well argue that true belief in God requires certain nurturing in faith schools, not neutral schools – rather as humanists may not want children being exposed to the lures of smoking.

Even if there is a presumption in favour of individuals' autonomy, there remain many problems. Libertarian emphasis is on rights over, or ownership of, ourselves and, by extension, our labour and property. The neutral state is then to be a minimal state protecting individuals; it is a night-watchman. The state may tax, that is, take money from individuals, to provide mutual protection, but it may not do so solely to benefit others, for that is akin to instituting slave labour. Liberals, in contrast, emphasize the enabling of individuals, through welfare and education, to realize their autonomy. The liberals' neutral state is less austere than the libertarians' minimal state.

The distinction between liberalism and libertarianism results from different perspectives on autonomy. The liberal perspective is that of *creation*: how to create autonomy, how to give people the power to make choices in their own interests. The state needs to provide people, as children, with education and encouragement, if they would otherwise not be provided for. The libertarian perspective is that of *preservation*: how to preserve autonomy. We have individuals already with rights over themselves; so we must not infringe them. Libertarianism, with its emphasis on rights, is sometimes seen as the politics of fear; liberalism has more welcoming arms to its fellow citizens.

Humanists typically straddle both camps. They are eager to enable people to become autonomous; they are also keen on preserving autonomy. Both camps may be seen as grounded in respect. Libertarians respect individuals' rights to what they are and have; liberals respect individuals' rights to become and have. There are, once again, conflicting values; and, once again, matters of degree. Individuals, when saving for the future, may be limiting their powers and choices today in order to provide powers and choices in the future – sometimes 'just in case' they hit on hard times. So, libertarians acknowledge *some* restrictions on the self of today. Governments that tax to provide welfare benefits are doubtless limiting the powers and choices of many today, yet to improve the powers and choices of others – and maybe of the taxed in years to come.

Humanist liberal–libertarian disagreements over what constitutes the appropriate extent of individuals' freedom should perhaps make humanists less surprised by religious believers' claims about individuals' freedoms. If you sincerely believe that abortion is akin to murder, you should be radically unhappy with laws that permit even one abortion, let alone millions – after all, the state should protect innocent human beings. Yet the neutral state would typically permit early abortions, placing a woman's freedom on this matter over – well, over what? Killing innocent human beings? The neutral state is unlikely to assent to that; its framework is to protect the innocent. The state would probably hold here that there are differences of basic beliefs, with regard to the status of the foetus, between which it cannot adjudicate; so it must be left to the individuals personally involved – though it may show some unease about this: witness today the various laws against late abortions in typical secular states.

It is usually the religious, because of strong beliefs on such personal matters, who seek restrictions on the behaviour of others, but it need not be. Those with certain political commitments offer ideals of the perfect citizen; they may resist the neutral state's starting point of individuals, as if isolated monads. Think of the ideals espoused by various totalitarian regimes, where people are pressed into community living.

We speak abstractly, when speaking of what the neutral state may think; but, continuing with the abstraction, the state may recognize fundamental disagreements as demonstrating that there is no overwhelming evidence either way on some questions. Such recognition justifies leaving matters to the individuals concerned. This applies, for example, to early abortions, but not to the killing of babies. Touching on another killing theme, most states in fact are far from neutral over voluntary euthanasia, voluntary euthanasia being deemed murder; but many humanists rightly argue in favour of neutrality here – for there are genuine and currently irresolvable differences between people's views.

Both the religious and the non-religious should argue their case, but, with no definitive outcome, the neutral state, if truly neutral, opts for non-interference. When the religious arguments on one side end up solely in terms of 'faith', then that should have no sway; but when the religious bring to bear considerations that non-believers would recognize, for example, the possibility of slippery slopes or pains suffered by foetuses, then the debate is on. Evidence and empathies change; hence, the final banning of fox-hunting in Britain arguably can be seen as the state finally grasping that such hunting involves unnecessary human-imposed suffering. Even when there is certainty over matters, individuals' freedoms may still override imposing the certainty. At times in Europe there would have been more or less universal conviction that Earth is flat, but the neutral state should not prohibit people saying otherwise – and should not threaten torture and death for such sayings.

Many religious believers would accept the above approach, feeling, at the very least, a little embarrassed at the Christian treatment of Galileo, when he suggested Earth orbited the sun. These believers accept the neutral state. It permits them to argue the case for their religious views; they are free to encourage others into the ways of God, ways that may prohibit believers from doing what the neutral state permits. Many other religious believers, however, insist that certain actions are of such significance that the state's neutrality should be overridden. Thus, these religious believers may seek to censor or censure criticism of religion, threaten death to blasphemers and close down abortion clinics. What can be said to such believers to encourage their support for the neutral state?

We may point to their self-interest. Muslims in the West would be worse off, were Western countries under Evangelical Christian law and customs; and Christians would be worse off under conservative Islamic law and customs. We could point out still further divisions within each faith. We may even mention Scientologists and other odd sects, and how all would be worse off within a state that imposed atheism. Hence, they are better off living in a neutral state than risking a religious or atheistic state that may prohibit their religious practices. The neutral state is the protective state; it ensures no party is oppressed or silenced by others. Being but a practical appeal, religious sects

'IF THE QUEEN HAD BEEN A BOY ...'

E. M. Forster (1879–1970), the British novelist, actively supported humanism. He shone as a liberal individualist, latterly, it is true, in the comfort of an Honorary Fellowship of King's College, Cambridge. He opposed religion, actively supported unilateral disarmament, freedom of speech and the abolition of capital punishment. More quietly, homosexual himself, he argued for the repeal of laws against homosexual practices. He was the star defence witness when, in 1960, the publishers of D. H. Lawrence's *Lady Chatterley's Lover* were prosecuted for its alleged obscenity. Many years earlier, he was championing the poetry of C. P. Cavafy which often dealt openly with homosexual eroticism, describing Cavafy delightfully as 'a Greek gentleman in a straw hat, standing absolutely motionless at a slight angle to the universe.'

Forster valued personal relationships, famously writing, 'If I had to choose between betraying my country and betraying my friend, I hope I should have the guts to betray my country.' He recognized these were muddling matters, commenting – for example – that tolerance is not a great eternally established divine principle, but 'just a makeshift, suitable for an over-crowded and over-heated planet'.

In 1969 he received the Order of Merit from Queen Elizabeth II. Standing at a slight angle to the universe no doubt, he observed, 'If the Queen had been a boy, I should have fallen in love with her.'

may accept it for the moment, but aspire, on one glorious day when their preferred religion dominates, to impose a religious state. People of the Book are fighting for eternal life. Their temporary acceptance of a neutral state may be justified, justified by an end in view. Is there an argument that could appeal to reason rather than pragmatics to justify the neutral state to religious believers?

The moral codes of religions often espouse justice and fairness. Hence, appeals could be thus. Muslims do not want to be oppressed by Christians – and Christians not by Muslims – so the just position is neutrality. This may, paradoxically, be supported by faith – the faith that many religions recognize as required for belief. Faith indicates that the belief is not solely a matter of evidence – so reason suggests that state neutrality is the only fair way of running things. A response could be, as ever, that what to the neutral state seems fair, to the religious seems wicked. One does not say that murderers and non-murderers should be treated in the same way – and the abortionist, for many theists, is a murderer. Further, even when one has some recognition of fairness in treatment – for example, with regard to freedom of speech – other values may secure a higher authority, for example, not being offensive to God. There is no way out for humanists than to stand up and be counted. The neutral state does place some values over others; free speech usually receives a higher priority than avoidance of offence, for example.

The public-private distinction and discriminations

Mill's Liberty Principle is often seen as generating the distinction between the public and private. We are in the public realm when affecting others, in very general ways. The terminology is unkind to clarity. When lovers canoodle in parks, pursuing the private and intimate, they canoodle in public. The public–private distinction is best understood by asking: how long should the long arm of the law be? Regarding what should the law be silent? The Liberty Principle raises those questions rather than answering them. To defend and promote individual freedom, laws control certain interactions between people, but not all. Liberal law speaks on the topic of people killing each other and, one hopes, will one day be sterner about noise pollution, but is silent about adults falling in love and the degree of philosophical argument people should engage – even though these latter may adversely and indirectly affect others.

We do possess a sense of the private as personal. Most of us would be horrified were we constantly on public view, exposed in thought, feelings and flesh. Such privacy we share at most with intimates, usually small in number. The neutral state respects or tolerates this, and hence restrains those theists who would otherwise intrude and impose their religious restrictions upon personal intimate lives, maybe to save people's souls from corruption through rock music, dance, lustful images and worse. Perhaps private intimate behaviour should be protected from public interference simply because it is private and intimate, though that would not automatically justify all such behaviour being permitted in public spaces.

With individual *belief* being a private matter, at least belief should not to be interfered with, though the expression of belief may, of course, require some restriction. However, some sects, religious or not, believe in collective responsibility – with individuals' salvation or true realization requiring the group as a whole holding the right beliefs. Further, some theists may be offended merely by knowing that some ungodly believing is happening next door. The neutral state simply has to insist that the prize of autonomy entails that concerns about putative collective responsibility, and distress at offence, possess no place in law.

Law, though, is not the sole restrictive power. People are often restricted, even tyrannized, by custom and by particular groups to which they belong. Groups restrict the freedom of members to varying degrees: some religions, of course, place heavy restrictions on women's dress. The neutral state needs at least to try to ensure that people who join restrictive groups do so freely and are free to leave; but should the neutral state involve itself in the conditions of membership set for people to join certain groups, institutions, companies? This question raises puzzles concerning when and which discriminations should be permitted.

Friends who play poker together should not be obliged to invite others; those questing love are not required to ignore their preferences in hair colour and curves – clear cases of the law's silence. So, why is the law vocal when it comes to employment and services, compelling theists to consider job applicants who, according to scriptures, engage in wicked activities such as homosexuality? For that matter, why force non-believers to accept employees who need special prayer times, garbs or dangling crosses? Religious sects and, indeed, non-believers' groups, consist of autonomous individuals. Should not the neutral state protect their existence, beliefs and discriminations – as it protects people's freedoms to choose poker players and lovers? Where love is concerned, I may discriminate against blondes; where employment is concerned, I may not. Why?

Humanism's neutrality, once again, has to muddle through. Compromises occur, resting uneasily on significance of belief, majority opinion, the extent of harm and the ethos generated. Medical professionals, religiously opposed to abortion, are freed from involvement in abortive procedures, yet British Catholic adoption agencies, deeply committed to traditional family units, must not discriminate against homosexual couples. And were humanist doctors to refuse fertility treatment to theists, well … Granting exemptions to those impressed by scriptural commands is surely discriminatory, for why should only religious sources generate exemptions? Deciding on the basis of depth of belief is also unhappy. It could permit groups with a Ku Klux Klan flavour spreading their anti-Semitism and other racist practices.

The best that the neutral state can do is adopt a pragmatic line, taking into account the reasoning for discriminations, the effect on others and the strength of belief – but giving none of these considerations always carte blanche top priority. The neutral state, though, cannot get away from the fact that it highly values individuals' autonomy and so must protect that autonomy from others who, in expressing their own autonomy, seek to override it. Restaurants that serve only Italian dishes offend no one; they do not prevent plenty of other restaurants from catering to other tastes – and they have reason to develop that speciality. However, employment agencies that refuse to register Jews typically have no good grounds for such discriminatory speciality; they restrict opportunities, and could well build up hatreds.

A background feature here, associated with the creation-preservation distinction above, is that laws often preserve some attitudes, yet seek to change others. The preservation may protect justified rights; the creation may attack the unjustified. But arguments rage over which are justified. Preserving parents' rights to pass assets to children and send them to private schools impedes the less fortunate gaining equality of educational opportunity. Yet, creating new laws that aim at enhancing individuals' autonomy through increased education may restrict others' autonomy. Another example: legislation promoting the rights of women may restrict men's rights to have men-only clubs.

Of course, attitudes change and are changed; reflection, context and new generations lead people to see things afresh. Humanists have to muddle through – that is, compare and contrast cases – their muddling being motivated by the secular spirit's promotion of autonomy, yet not at any cost. Compassion, for example, also merits an important place.

Democracy: votes and vetoes

People's autonomy suggests that they should have a say in determining the laws, some that uphold, and some that restrict, autonomy. This is a justification for individuals' rights to vote – that is, to engage in procedures that lead to collective decisions relating to government and law. That people participate and value participation – and that they deliberate on the options – is as important as the particular means whereby the collective decisions are reached. Humanists typically promote democracy. 'Democracy', though, is these days a term of approval; yet it embraces myths, confusions and dangers.

If democracy is merely rule by the majority – at least individuals making up that majority thereby secure some sort of autonomy – then we face the danger of the majority tyrant, a danger that much exercised Mill, despite such tyranny possibly securing happiness maximization. Minorities may find themselves ignored, oppressed, even dismissed from democratic procedures. The majority may vote for laws against homosexual practices and against immigrants receiving welfare. So, majority rule needs to be constrained, for democracy involves democratic rights and hence rights of minorities. Democracy, it is argued, is grounded in equality of respect for individuals' autonomy, thus in harmony with humanism's values.

Humanity's dignity requires not just the vote (for), but the veto (against). Both elements can be justified from an impartial perspective. Standing outside, detached, we may reasonably feel the only way to decide something is to add up votes *for*, thus running the dangers of minorities' oppression. Standing outside, detached, we may yet empathize with each individual and see therefore the power of a justified veto *against*, thus protecting minorities, but frustrating the majority by the tyranny of minority rights.

'Rights' talk is a way of expressing vetoes or trump cards, in recognition of happiness, flourishing, as grounded in distinct individuals. Maximizing happiness is maximizing each individual's happiness rather than an undifferentiated happiness mass that could just happen to reside in a few lucky people. Once we have individual people as units, we have no good reason to dismiss respect for some, rather than others, as autonomous agents. Of course, vetoes only work when there is a respect for vetoes; trump cards can only be played when the game is in play. Sometimes, though, the institution of vetoing, the existence of the game itself, may be under threat – as in extreme emergencies such as war. What then is to be done?

There is no easy calculus – indeed, no calculus at all – for working out when and to what extent, for example, the right to free speech should be overridden by the right to protect citizens, or when it is right for political leaders to dirty their moral hands. Further, recent tendencies to multiply rights endanger the significance of rights. We may sit up sharp, when some proposed action is seen as threatening the right to life – but when seen as threatening my right to my pencil or two weeks' paid holiday? Rights enshrined in law may be justified as means of individuals' protection. Rights talk, though, is highly inappropriate for many relationships. To insist on rights and duties flowing from being in love may well undermine that love: think of the unease many people feel at prenuptial contracts.

Democracy is grounded in treating individuals equally with regard to rights, and there is often emphasis on people being equal. Of course, casual talk of 'everyone being equal' is simply false, if literally read. We differ in myriad ways and also merit numerous differences in treatment. It is silly to insist that people with broken legs should receive the same treatment as those unbroken. Maybe there should be equal concern for everyone securing an autonomous and flourishing life – the typical humanist stance – but does such equal concern justify taxing the wealthy to help the poor? Our humanist fellow feeling says 'yes'; but only so far … Is equal concern for all most likely to come about, in practice, through democratic machinery? Well, who can be sure?

'Equality of opportunity' tends to be the current cry – from humanists and non-humanists alike – rather than equality of outcome. People pay lip service to children having the same educational opportunity, while ensuring that their children receive advantages of private education and inherited wealth. In fact, the whole enterprise of 'equality of opportunity' is conceptually flawed: does having an equal start require equality in intellectual ability, motivation, genetic inheritance, money – or what? Another example: how is fairness manifested? Should speeding fines be a fixed sum of money? Surely, fairness answers 'yes'. Or does it? The fixed sum is hardly noticed by the wealthy, yet hugely noticed by the poor. How do we judge on such matters? Whatever answers are given, why those rather than others? Humanists, as do others, end up living lives that embrace the conceptually flawed and uncertain.

Unjustified inequalities have sometimes been identified as those which do not result from people's choices and do not help the worse off to become better. Such inequalities, the argument goes, should be overcome by some redistribution of goods; thus, programmes of positive discrimination are justified – for example, greater opportunities for socially disadvantaged children. This can sound so right. But now reflect on the considerable inequality of male-female life expectancies, an inequality that benefits neither men nor women. Should steps be taken to iron out the inequality, maybe by improved health services or reduced working hours for men compared with women? Curiously, this proposal meets with no widespread approval, suggesting that which features we take as significant when seeking equalities, deciding rights and choosing priorities must have other values – or prejudices – at play.

Apart from such fundamental problems, there are many curiosities in democratic practices with which humanists live. Minimally, humanists' promotion of autonomy suggests equality with regard to votes counting. In practice though, and with protection of minorities to one side, many Western democracies have little regard for the majority vote. Most elections are but snapshots of electoral choices between political packages determined by very small minorities. Governments, because of constituency structures, are frequently elected on a minority of the votes of those who bothered to vote. So, when politicians speak of election results demonstrating the will of the people, they are usually mischievous.

People, to be autonomous, should be reflective and well informed when visiting polling stations, the aim being to decide what collectively should be done, but in practice many are voting with regard to self-interest; some are not. As for the electorate being well informed, much information is by way of slick advertisements determined by political wealth, and crude misleading headlines encouraged by a few non-elected powerful editors. Humanists, naturally, are much concerned by all this. A particular focus is the role of religious pressure groups on government. Special government ears listen to such groups, but not so much to the secular and humanist. Humanists sensibly aspire to level playing fields on such matters, but – of course – they cannot prevent theists from voting according to religious beliefs, beliefs that may restrict non-believers' freedoms. All that humanists can do is appeal to the reasonableness of the theists, but reasonableness is sometimes in short supply.

Democracy's emphasis on autonomy receives expression in the promotion of free speech, for both speakers and hearers, a free speech available even to those who are eager to restrict free speech. As Forster implies, free speech is required for democracy – and, we should add, free speech is not worth much, if people's ears are blocked. Free speech has distinctive merit in helping people to flourish. Roughly, what is said will involve either truths or falsehoods or both. To the extent that truth is present, the speech should be welcomed – for we are more likely to secure flourishing lives if in touch with truth rather than error, a point made when considering a sailing example in the chapter to come. To the extent that what is said is false, then it should stimulate those possessing the truth into defending that truth, explaining their reasons and acting in accord with the truth.

Theists often insist on how offensive they find certain speech, when the Lord's name is taken in vain. Thus, we encounter blasphemy laws and censorship. The humanist response is that the value of free speech outweighs any offence caused. 'Dear Religious Believer,' we may say, 'you believe as you do because you think you have hold of the truth; but securing that truth required the freedom of enquiry, of speculation, of expression. To prefer a state that blocks these when unfavourable to you is to undermine commitment to truth's value.' Preparedness to challenge beliefs is essential to our humanity's reasoning, though I, for one, begin to have some doubts about media freedoms, when newspaper headlines wilfully misrepresent the truth and stir up nasty campaigns. Perhaps in some cases, newspapers' banners should label them as 'myth-papers' rather than news.

Although democracy, in view of caveats above, merits only two cheers, if even the two, at least the neutral state encourages people to flourish – to conduct, in Mill's words, 'experiments in living', to live their lives as they reflectively wish. For humanists, the neutral state deserves the full three cheers.

Let us not, though, run away with the 'three cheers' as suggesting that, fundamentally, all can be easy-going in the neutral state. Humanists face conflicts in their thinking, especially when emergencies arise – as will be seen in Chapter 8.

6
Dying and living

'Tis better to be a dissatisfied Socrates than a satisfied pig.

John Stuart Mill

In life, there is death – the death of others; the anticipation of our own. Encountering death opens eyes on life. How should we handle death – and life, and creation of life and hence sex? Humanists have no instruction book, no preachers to whom to turn; but we may review some humanist considerations. Three teeny vignettes follow:

Melissa is a young woman, at university, a bright future ahead; she's finally facing the fact of her pregnancy, father unknown. She feels dreadful at the idea of abortion. Were she to have the child, her parents would be supportive, yet she knows full well that it would affect her career, her future relationships, her whole way of life. Melissa does not want to be a mother so early on.

Charles has a wasting, painful disease. Already he can hardly move. He recognizes his life is drawing to an end. Suffering additional years, paralysed, needing personal care day and night, is not his idea of a good end to life. Euthanasia is illegal where he lives; but he asks his son to help him to die, by taking him abroad where assisted suicide and euthanasia are legally permitted.

Mrs Jones seems fortunate to the outside world. A well-respected schoolteacher, she is comfortably off, with a successful accountant husband and two children at college. Yet, now forty, she feels an emptiness within her soul. She sees the trappings of middle-class suburban existence as – *trappings*. She's tempted by another man, bringer of colour and life into her life. She could have a secret affair. Maybe she might even 'up and go'; he has contacts in southern France, in an artists' community – with artists who live for their art, their sexuality, the sun. If she doesn't get out soon, she never will.

To appreciate such dilemmas, think yourself into the feelings and thoughts – get under the skin – of a Melissa, a Charles or Mrs Jones. Dilemmas demand not merely intellectual grasp; they require imagination and empathy – and more detail. They need the heartbeats of everyday living, vivid description, or thought-provoking fiction. Arguably, this is why simple moral principles often fail to connect with real-life decisions. They shimmer thinly in abstract heavens rather than gaining nourishment from life here on earth.

When grappling with dilemmas, we grapple with what sort of people we are – and will be. And even if we uphold certain fixed moral values – perhaps we believe it wrong ever to take life, break a promise or abandon our children – we may yet wonder whether we *should* step beyond those values. Morality is not automatically overriding. Some describe such dilemmas as 'ethical', where ethics embraces more values than the moral. Morality tends to be associated with duties and principles; 'ethics' highlights how we may wrestle with who we are, with what weight we give to morality in our lives, with which life we identify – with whether we can live with ourselves, having abandoned a family, let down our father or chosen an abortion. Although the big dilemmas of death and life impress our thoughts, we frequently manifest who we are by the small and seemingly insignificant. Little everyday courtesies, kindness and thoughtfulness – they matter too. Humanists, dare I say, when on trains, would not rest their dirty shoes on seats opposite.

The eternal recurrence

The greatest weight recurs. Nietzsche asked whether we would welcome our lives being repeated eternally, exactly the same each time round. The eternal recurrence – this most dreadful and anguishing of thoughts, albeit nonsensical – is intended to concentrate our minds on how we should live, on what life we value. Are you someone who thinks it right to end a life? Could you live a life – and be well disposed to yourself – in which you abandoned your children?

Life, it is said and said somewhat casually, is sacred, precious, of the greatest importance. For many, humanists included, this amounts to everyone possessing the right to life. The accompanying duty is not to take life. The right and duty are flimsy, when they impose so few demands – for the duty never to take life is rarely identified with the duty to save life whenever possible. The dispossessed and starving of the world would, I suspect, prefer food to rights, shelter to tales of how sacred are their lives, and opportunities to flourish rather than prayers from the wealthy. Humanism deletes the prayers, but confronts the ubiquitous problem – of our being concerned for the whole of humanity, yet not *that* concerned.

We are thinking no doubt of *human* lives, the right to life existing in virtue of being human, yet why discriminate against non-human creatures? With humanism the topic, we have freely interchanged 'humans' and 'persons'. We need, though, to meet the charge of speciesism. We are speciesist, if we discriminate purely on the basis of species; such discrimination is perhaps akin to racism and sexism. The key is not really discrimination, but unjustified discrimination. We need to identify relevant features – morally relevant features – to justify our lesser interest in non-humans. Striped or spotted, winged or finned – such differences lack any obvious relevance to whether caging and killing are morally right, unless more is said. The more may be 'capacity to suffer', for that gives rise to a moral 'ought not': we ought not to cause gratuitous suffering. And now we see that the 'ought not' fans out to non-human creatures, for they can suffer. Humanistic concern hence extends beyond humans. Suffering, though, is not the sole moral factor. Were it so, then killing people painlessly could be morally fine.

The humanist interest in human beings' dignity is an interest in individuals as the source of value. Individuals may identify what is worthy of being desired, what is valuable in itself, what is important. For example, people see friendships and fairness as highly desirable. People themselves are also valuable, not least because they possess this reflective awareness of what is valuable. A person usually considers his own life as valuable. Most of us also value love and eroticisms, lusts and longings. Of course, to be individuals who can decide what is desirable, important, valuable, does not require that they are always doing the deciding – any more than to be a plumber involves plumbing each moment. Valuing one's life requires the *capacity* to be aware of oneself, one's continuing life, as something one values. Let us restrict use of 'persons' for those individuals who possess such capacity.

Arguably, most, if not all, non-humans lack the capacity to value their own lives; and so it is easier to justify killing them than persons. In killing non-person creatures, we are not disvaluing what they value, though we may, of course, be causing distress to others. In killing persons, we are usually destroying something they value – their own lives – and so, such killing is usually morally wrong. Persons, given this specific understanding, possess a right to life that non-person creatures lack. That is, typically we have a duty not to take the lives of persons. We may still think non-person lives are important. We may value them for themselves, without needing to value them as valuers or only as means to human ends. (Chapter 9 says more about non-human animals, their valuing or not, and the alleged human superiority.)

It is on the cards that some non-human creatures are persons – chimps, dolphins, Martians (hypothetical self-aware creatures from other planets), spring to mind. Also, it seems, some humans are not persons, for example arguably those in persistent vegetative states, with no capacity any longer for consciousness at all. Human corpses are not persons. In everyday use, 'humans' typically means persons – and, as a matter of fact, most adult humans are persons and most persons are humans – so we shall continue to follow common usage, except when the distinction is important for the argument, as tends to be the case in this chapter. After all, if we resisted common usage, we should probably be speaking of personism rather than humanism and become trapped in other unhappy expressions.

With the distinction between humans and persons currently in mind though, we can see that it is as persons that we reflect on our lives, on morality, on how to treat others. And the eternal recurrence reminds us that we do choose how to live our lives, at least to some extent. Even when we let ourselves be swept along by events, we are doing the letting. Whether we metaphysically possess free will or not, we frequently make choices: you may choose to turn the page – or not. Humanism draws attention to our responsibility in choice making. We should not – and, indeed, cannot – pass the moral buck.

Sartre tells of a student who sought advice. They were in 1940s Paris, under German occupation. The student faced a choice: should he escape to England, join the Free French Forces in order to return to the continent and fight, helping to combat tyranny? Or, should he stay in Paris to look after his mother? She lived alone, lived only for him; she was in despair, her elder son, the pupil's brother, having been killed. The student wanted to avenge that death; yet he recognized the needs of his mother. He felt for her, was devoted to her. The project of fighting was an ambiguous action in that it 'might vanish like water into sand and serve no purpose', whereas everything he did for his mother would aid her to live. Advisers may say various things, yet the student had to choose which advisers to seek and how to weigh their words. He may choose on the basis of feelings, but he needs then to weigh his feelings. Sartre's comment is: 'You are free, therefore choose – that is to say, invent.'

Sartre's tale is often taken to show that all values derive through our choices – the world is without value until we choose – yet the tale does not obviously show that. The student is already recognizing many values: the significance of a mother's need, the evils of tyranny and the importance of his brother's death. His dilemma arises because those existent recognized values compete for his action. To choose simply on the basis of some dice or chance, as in Luke Rhinehart's *The Dice Man*, would make his choosing appear trivial, the choice capricious. He wants to make the right choice. And, in his choice, he will, in a sense, be making himself.

That there is a choice is right, but that it is a choice made without reason is wrong. Discussion may bring out more about the likelihood of success in joining the resistance; more discussion could show other possibilities for the mother. Thinking through the details may cast the options in different lights. The descriptions used may help him spot his true motivations. 'You'd face a coward in the mirror each day you stayed at home. This is so, isn't it?' 'Yes, but that could be the courageous path.' At that, he may realize that his motivation for leaving is the ignoble one of fearing humiliation as a coward, if remaining with his mother. Courage is needed to overcome fear.

In literary contexts, F. R. Leavis spoke of discussion having the form, 'This is so, is it not?' being met by 'Yes, but ...' Dialogue, reflection, comparisons and contrasts – these all form part of reasoning in dilemmas; and although such reasoning lacks formal deductive or inductive structures, it is not thereby ruled out as good reasoning. As John Wisdom would point out, in courts of law, judges weigh up the evidence, concluding that the defendant was negligent or acted unreasonably. In dilemmas of the ethical and moral variety, there may often be agreement; but, as suggested at Chapter 4's end, in some cases two people in the same circumstances may reach conflicting decisions about what it is right to do and, in a sense, be right in their decision. Perhaps that is the message to derive from Sartre's tale: one student could be right to live a life devoted to his mother; another right to go and fight – yet, but for that decision and their subsequent lives, they need not have differed.

And this again brings out how persons may make their own lives, how they may create their moral selves – a key element in humanism's value of persons.

To display some further considerations in humanist valuations, relevant to subsequent dying and living dilemmas, we turn to the oceans.

You, a young man, want to sail round the world single-handedly. The idea appeals, as does the fame – and the likelihood of women throwing themselves at such bronzed, weather-beaten, sea-dog courage. Of course, you won't ever set sail: it requires considerable skill; you are prone to seasickness and cannot swim. This is, though, your lucky day. You have the option to plug into an experience machine, a vastly superior virtual reality machine. Just plug in, and you will get all the experiences – all the thrills and spills – of worldwide sailing, with the experiences of praise and ravishing kisses at the end. Once plugged, your experiences will strike you as real. You will not know that you are on the machine; you will not remember getting plugged. There will be all the sensations of danger, of crashing waves, of storms and leaks, and then the final roaring success. Would you plug in? Disregard the practical 'if's and 'but's; the machine is guaranteed safe.

Many choose the plugging – and that may well be right on occasions – but does the machine really give you all that you want in wanting to sail round the world? What we value for ourselves is not just experiences, not just how things strike us, but also our relationship to the world, even though, in a sense, all we have are our experiences. You want to sail round the world, not merely have the experiences *as if* sailing – even though, on the machine, you cannot tell the difference between the reality and illusion. You want the achievement, not mere appearance of achievement.

There are numerous experiences that we enjoy or want. You may well like the sensualities of sex, the taste of champagne and the freshness of ocean winds biting your face; and the sensations alone may often be worthy of desire. But they are usually tied in with other valuable things that cannot be reduced to the experiential alone. You want there to be a real person, maybe one you love, engaged in your eroticism. You want to be sharing the champagne with friends, really there, as you talk the sun down. When we choose how to live, we seek not solely experiences, but contact with reality, with attaining the truth, with achieving the goal. Ignorance is not always bliss; or, if it is, bliss is not all that we value. Achievement is not the experience *as if* of achievement; courage is not the experience as if of courage. And although these examples have all been to do with what individuals value directly for themselves, it is, of course, also important how well things go for others, independently of their effects on us.

Suppose some young people are involved in accidents and become brain damaged: as a result, they forget their past, have only desires for sweets and sleep, the satisfaction of which provides them with swathes of delight. Were all satisfactions equal in value, we should applaud their new lives. Or, drawing on Plato, we spray people with itching powder, thereby giving them continual opportunities for scratching satisfactions. For Mill – and, surely, for us – we see the lives of the brain-damaged and the scratchers as far removed from flourishing. ''Tis better to be a dissatisfied Socrates than a satisfied fool or pig.' Mill's comment should stop in their tracks those who see his utilitarianism as nothing but a satisfaction theory. A flourishing life is more than a series of pleasurable episodes.

Harming the dead and dying

Humanists take death to be annihilation. The body remains as corpse and gradually breaks up, or more swiftly, if enflamed. Consciousness, experiences – they all cease. In view of this, humanism often warms to Epicurus. 'When death is there, we are not; when we are there, death is not.' We have nothing to fear in death for once dead we no longer exist. True, we may be unhappy now at the thought of not living on and unhappy at others living on beyond us – maybe we are anxious about their suffering, maybe we have some vague notion of the injustice – but when we are dead, we are nothing. So, why should humanists be worried about dead people, save in as far as the deaths distress the living?

The experience machine experiment should set our thinking aright. Not all harms are experiential harms. Suppose Miranda values her family life, the fidelity of her husband. Suppose, though, that her husband has numerous affairs, yet feigns faithfulness. Suppose too that her children lack respect for her, but pretend otherwise. Suppose all these things and also that Miranda never finds out. Is she not being harmed? She never finds out; but were she to find out, she would be highly distressed. Now, the distress need not be at finding out. Finding out could be useful in making changes to her life. She would be distressed at what she found out about, namely, that she was betrayed. That is a harm she has undergone, her interests damaged. The harm exists, even though she is unaware of the betrayal – even though she is unaware that she has been harmed.

That is all very well and good – if sad – but does it provide a foothold for harms occurring to the dead? Miranda exists to be harmed; the deceased no longer exist. Corpses are not people, yet we are respectful in their presence, and horrified by those who mutilate them for fun. We respect deathbed wishes. Perhaps these things tell us something about what sort of people we are; but that cries out for an explanation. Why is treatment of the dead morally significant for humanists?

Here is an answer. The deceased were once people – valuers – and people's interests extend beyond their experiences and biological life. Our mother tells us, in April, just before she dies, how important it is *to her* that we respect her last requests. Now, she is deceased and we are in June. If we ignore her wishes, are we harming her? Certainly she does not exist now, here in June; but what we do now may still harm the mother who once lived. Were the mother to find out – true, an impossibility – she would be distressed at our lack of respect.

The big and special case of harm is that of death and being dead. Relatives of the deceased are often highly distressed, distressed not just at *their* loss of loved ones. They are distressed at the loss of life – the deprivation of future years – suffered by the now deceased. Can humanists make sense of that?

We return to Miranda, supposing she is twenty-five years old. She goes swimming off Rio de Janeiro's Ipanema Beach late one night. Unfortunately, she encounters Suzie, aged five. Suzie is a shark, well disposed to human flesh and soon well fed on Miranda. Miranda no longer exists; so how can she have been harmed by her death? The way forward is this: compare Miranda's actual life of twenty-five years, before Suzie's dining, with the realistically possible life of eighty years. That identifies the loss of fifty-five years that she has suffered, even though she knows nothing of it. We also have grip on our greater distress, common when a person dies young than when old. After all, if I, aged ninety-nine, go swimming off Ipanema Beach early one morning and Suzie attacks, clearly desperate for something to eat and lacking aesthetic discrimination, few people feel my loss is as great as Miranda's.

The above discussion is controversial. However, once we have the foothold of existence, to use a phrase from Henry Salt, we can make sense of how we could live for longer than we in fact do, without losing who we are. Arguably, though, we cannot make sense of how our lives could have started considerably earlier than they did. If this asymmetry exists, then it answers Lucretius, who claimed, in supporting Epicurus, that we should no more fear the loss of life after death than regret the lack of life before birth. Humanists, although believing death to be annihilation, need not, as we now see, follow the Epicurean path. Even though there is no sense in worrying about harming those never born, death remains a harm. It may not, however, be as bad as continuing with intense suffering; so, we now turn to the deliberate ending of life that is euthanasia.

Euthanasia is the killing of people, for their own sake – in their interests. Voluntary euthanasia occurs when the people request death. One thing humanists will not do is object to voluntary euthanasia on the grounds of life being God's gift or the divine command never to kill, curiously a command readily violated in war and even by God. Humanists are also disinclined to admire the religious reasoning that can permit deliverance of lethal injections to reduce suffering, with the death merely foreseen not intended. Once the intended–foreseen distinction is in play, we have scope for contested application in other cases. We should not, of course, condone the man who knows he has HIV, yet still has unprotected sex with someone unknowing and uninfected. Yet he defends his action, for he merely foresaw the possibility of infection transmission; he intended to provide love and pleasure. This HIV love example should at least make casual players of the intended–foreseen distinction say a fair bit more to show the distinction is morally relevant.

Humanists value people making their own choices about important things in their lives. Turning to our Charles example, his life and how it ends are vitally important to him. We may know that his wishes are not transient yens. No wonder-drug will cure him; no palliative care will help. Put ourselves in his shoes. Choosing how to live our life may well vitally involve choosing how and when to die. There are factors to be weighed. Charles's children may be distressed, though they should also consider the distress to Charles, if pressing him to live on.

Of course, there are borderline cases and changes of mind, but there are clear cases when people have had enough. Not everything about the living human condition rates the accolade of 'dignity'. For many, constant pain, double incontinence, muscle decay – and much more – may make living not worth the candle. Surely, no person of compassion would insist on individuals having to undergo a life that they truly do not want in such circumstances. Some would argue that Charles's decision is devaluing *all* life, recommending that others in his position should do likewise. That is an error. Charles is not legislating for others.

Humanists can have no objection to voluntary euthanasia on direct moral grounds – and obviously not on religious grounds. Objections, if objections are due, have to be made on other grounds. The clinching factor for some humanists and theists alike, with theists now taking an interest in unintended consequences, is the slippery slope. With voluntary euthanasia morally approved, we may slide into approving the involuntary. That slide certainly is not conceptually justified. There is a radical difference between voluntary and involuntary requests. Maybe the objection is that, as a matter of empirical fact, the permissibility of voluntary euthanasia would lead people into having less respect for life, leading to pressures on the elderly to agree to euthanasia and maybe society deciding when it is best for people to die, imposing involuntary death on them (as, according to theists, God often does). But why are people so sure that is how things will develop?

Most societies permit voluntary sexual intercourse. They do not argue that, because of such acceptance, there will be a slide down the slippery slope, leading through 'well, all right then' sex, reluctant sex – to date rapes, acquaintance rapes and finally clear and violent rapes as morally permissible, even demanded. That there are grey areas about what is voluntary or involuntary does not show that there are not clear cases on either side.

Similar questions arise with non-voluntary euthanasia, that is, with people in states such that they cannot express their wishes. Many humanists support advance directives, so that people can make clear how they want to be treated, if in such states. We may add that cases referred to as those of 'persistent vegetative states' should properly be understood as cases in which the person no longer exists, only the biological human body. In such cases, in whose interests can it possibly be to leave the body alive, yet psychologically void? Would most people, if they reflected on the matter, truly value their life continuing in that way and, indeed, using up medical resources utterly without point? Many humanists may doubt it.

Living: abortion and sexual relations

In valuing life, many people – though not all – value having children, and, in due course, the children having children. Mind you, it is far from clear that, if you value those who live, you should therefore value their creation. Humanists do, of course, typically value children as much as do theists, though arguably humanists pay more attention to having only children whose lives are likely to go well. The opposition by some religions to artificial contraception and abortion strikes many humanists as cruel and inconsistent. It is cruel because, as a result, some babies are born to live for a few months or years racked with pain and disability and then die without having had any valuable experiences. Let us stress, just because many of us would support abortion of radically damaged foetuses, it does not follow that we do not value people who are disabled. Here is an analogy. People who support some degree of sexual abstinence do not thereby disvalue people who are living.

The religious attitude against contraception is inconsistent because if sexual abstinence is permitted, and various forms of pregnancy-avoiding rhythm methods are permitted, then the moral feature has to rest upon contraception's artificiality or unnaturalness. But just because something is unnatural, in the sense of involving some human intent or contrivance, it cannot possibly follow, or be evidence for, that thing or activity being wrong. Operating theatres, bicycles and (maybe) controlling one's anger are unnatural, but highly desirable. Measles, monsoons and premature mortality are highly natural, but not thereby desirable.

One significant matter that many encounter in their lives is that of abortion. Abortion for some is enmeshed within their religious belief in such a way that it is deemed immediately to be an evil. So, let us run through some humanist thinking on this highly charged subject.

Humanists, of course, have no truck with magical dates, be they those of conception, three days after, or fourteen days later, when fertilized eggs, according to some, allegedly are ensouled. How could we possibly tell when ensoulment occurs? Further, that human fertilized eggs are human says nothing immediately morally relevant, for what is prima facie morally wrong is killing persons, whereas human foetuses, at least for many, many weeks, are not persons: recall our understanding of 'persons' above. Unborn babies are no more babies than incomplete circles are circles.

The line usually taken by abortion opposers – including some humanists as well as many theists – is that fertilized eggs possess the potential for personhood. That is true, but having the potential to be X does not warrant the same treatment as that due to X. Acorns should not be treated as oak trees and heirs to thrones lack sovereigns' rights. People have the potential to be corpses, but are not thereby to be treated as corpses when alive.

Were the 'potential' anti-abortion argument to stand, we ought to object equally to contraception and sexual abstinence. Jack and Jill's mutual glancings could lead to sexual intercourse, a baby, child, adult with a happy life resulting. But, surely, nobody would object to Jill's refusing sex with Jack; well, no one should object on the grounds that her refusal prevents a future happy person's existence. Within Jack and Jill there are cells with the potential to bring about a person. Resistance to the flirtatious glances could block the realization. It is no good answer to say that egg and spermatozoon have not yet come together so there is no single item with the potential to be a person. That is, as I have quipped elsewhere, to be space-ist and number-ist. Just because there is space between the relevant egg and spermatozoon, it fails to follow that the twosome lacks potential.

Rejection of typical 'potential' arguments does not imply that abortion is an easy moral matter. It is not. And although some religious believers are committed to all abortions being so wrong that they should never be performed, many in the anti-abortion camp make exceptions, when the pregnancy results from rape or when the pregnant female is very young. And most in the pro-abortion camp feel considerable unease at late abortions. Many rightly believe that, in contrast to murder, abortion is not a black or white issue; this is because biology involves gradual development. There is a gradual development from glancers (so to speak) to fertilized eggs to embryos to foetuses to babies to children to adults ... to corpses.

Although an item's possessing the potential to be X does not make it X, we recognize the moral significance of an item's being closer to realization of its potential. If X is valued, we value those items that have almost achieved X-status more than those items a long way off. Perhaps this is to do with how likely it is that X will be achieved. Billions of sexual intercourses and billions of fertilized eggs, even without contraception or deliberate abortion, would not lead to people coming into existence. We usually have no good reason to believe that a particular contraceptive use is likely to prevent the existence of a person who, but for the contraception, would definitely come about. We do have very good reason to believe that a late abortion of a healthy foetus is highly likely to prevent the existence of a person who, but for the abortion, would come about. This offers some justification for the perceived moral difference between contraception, early and late abortions. That there is the gradual development should give pause to those bishops who speak of abortions as massacres and murderous killings, akin to those of shootings in Dunblane or Virginia. Such claims are mistaken. To liken women who have abortions, perhaps after much anguishing, perhaps even after rapes, to murderers is horrendous and demonstrates little humanity. Humanists would not do that.

Many arguments concerning abortion hang on rights: the rights of the woman over her body; the rights of the unborn child. In a seminal article, Judith Jarvis Thomson argued that, even if the foetus is a person with a right to life, it does not follow that the mother has no right to remove it from her body as, so to speak, a trespasser. The foetus's right to life is not thereby a right to everything required for life. After all, someone, unconnected with me, in some remote part of the world, does not obviously have a *right* to one of my kidneys, even if it is only my kidney that would save her. Declaring rights as part of the natural order is, as we have heard from Bentham, nonsense on stilts; rather we need to see how rights come about through various human activities.

If I have promised my kidney, then the would-be recipient has a right to expect it. If a couple engage in sexual intercourse, without contraception, and if – *if* – foetuses were persons, then, arguably and metaphorically, any resultant foetus may possess a right to be carried. Thomson correctly emphasizes, though, that even if the foetus (as a person) has no right to use of the woman's body, it does not follow that the woman is right to have an abortion. Morality, or at least ethics, extends beyond rights, or what is just, into areas to do with being kind, compassionate and courageous – and what sort of life we should be proud to live. Recall the virtue ethics of Chapter 4.

What should our Melissa do? Humanism would have no party line on this – and that is surely right. More details are needed and Melissa needs to weigh up how the various factors affect her and how she sees her life and family. Humanists would urge her to make her decision on the basis of accurate beliefs, not poor arguments about potentiality or God popping in souls; but, given the emotional impact that abortion often has, what to do may still be no easy decision. Humanists would probably stress that it is her decision. What could she live with? What sort of life does she want to lead and what sort could she be pleased about?

The question of how to live a life and what sort of life one should lead is also very much in focus for the religious when sex is on the agenda. So, let us turn to some simple humanist-orientated points on this topic.

Religion is hung up over sex. Most of us are hung up over sex, one way or another. A variety of sexual codes and taboos have come and gone, many explained by religious belief, some by circumstances. Once again, one thing that unites humanists is that scholarly debates about what the scriptures mean, what the Church or Mosque traditionally believes and what, according to theists, God has revealed, are all without point, save as ways of bringing out just what some people do believe and feel on these matters. That sincere Christians, for example, reach opposite views on the morality of homosexuality should lead them to conclude it is a personal matter. Individuals should judge for themselves: live and let live.

The humanist stance tends to be that, in as far as sexual activity does not adversely affect non-consenting others, then it is a private matter and people should be free to do as they judge best – having regard, of course, to numerous moral factors, including dignity, integrity, respect for oneself as well as for others. Bentham, in defending homosexual behaviour, made the point, made bravely for his times, that one should be allowed to scratch

'HELL IS OTHER PEOPLE'

Jean-Paul Sartre (1905–1980), the French philosopher and novelist, may seem far removed from humanism, in announcing that hell is other people. At one stage, though, he explicitly aligned himself to humanism and, throughout his life, he was certainly humanistic, in that he denied the existence of God, valued human beings – and fought a range of injustices. Where Sartre differs from many of today's humanists is in his existentialist belief that it is our choices which show what is valuable and, in some way, create those values. According to Sartre, human beings do not possess a nature or essence, save that of having to make free choices. We are condemned to be free.

Why are other people hell? Well, Sartre stresses how others try to categorize or objectify us. We may even do that ourselves, when pretending we are forced to act in a certain way or be of a certain type. That, for Sartre, is to engage in bad faith, to be inauthentic. Sartre, then, clearly values our not denying our freedom and responsibility in choice.

In the end, other people win: once we are dead, we can no longer create ourselves. We are at the mercy of the assessment by others, by the Other.

where it itches. Intrusions by custom, the law and religious doctrine, prohibiting the kaleidoscope of consensual sexual activities that tempt many – from leather to love – would typically lack obvious justification. Of course, sexual activity is not, so to speak, a casual affair: in as far as it may produce children, obligations are clearly generated. Sexual activity is also no casual affair, in that it can be deeply significant in human relationships.

Morality enters into sexual matters, for most humanists, not because of anything distinctive about sexual morality, but because of typical moral concerns about our treatment of others and how we respect ourselves. Sexual relations, as with numerous other relationships, can give rise to distressing jealousies, obsessions that may ruin lives and simple dangers of disease. All these possibilities need, as ever, to be weighed up against other valuable features: the pleasures, the explorations, the commitments and bondings. Promiscuity, to use an old-fashioned term, is not morally wrong in itself, according to typical humanists, though this is one example where there are, for some people, still very different feelings about men's sexual activity and women's – and where women can often feel abused because of their sex and their stance over sex.

Even if not harming others, many – Mill, for example – would think of lives dominated by sexual lusts and activities as more akin to swinish living. Arguably, to live well, to be proud of our lives, many of us feel the need for more than simply satisfying lusts – be they for the intoxications of sex, alcohol or sleep. Yet such intoxications surely merit a place in many good lives, and it is not at all impossible that some may find personal development, fulfilment and creativity, through deep involvement in the skirmishes of erotic investigations. It is true that sex simply for the sake of sexual release may not typically be as significant as sex within deep romance and love; but relationships come in various degrees, with various features and potentials – and circumstances, age and commitments affect how sexual encounters are perceived and develop.

As ever in life, there are balances and balances, compromises and compromises, 'if's and 'but's. Humanism recognizes that these are personal decisions – for individuals to make about how they want their lives to develop, taking into account others. They are not decisions that are aided by the guilt, anguishing and repressions encouraged by many religious doctrines.

Only connect!

People readily connect with each other, though the connections – humanists rightly see – can be disturbed and warped by beliefs supernatural and superstitious. Connections, however, may also be enhanced by religious belief, something that humanists are not so keen to see. Viewing life as a gift may be a poetical way of valuing life. Viewing the world as sacred may be an attachment to many natural splendours – to other species as well as the environment. Humanists have these attachments, with recourse neither to the divine, nor language of the divine.

Deepest connections typically arise through family life, through erotic love – through friendships, projects and interests. There are strengths here as well as fragilities. There are also partialities. One cannot be impartial concerning whom one loves or whose company one enjoys. And when other species enter the fray, one cannot be – and arguably should not be – so impartial that one seriously considers saving a drowning dog rather than a drowning person; or, indeed, whether one should first save from the flames an original Picasso painting rather than a stranger. Yet muddles and conflicts persist. One should save the person, not the painting. However, we deploy resources to fund artists and purchase Old Masters, resources that could otherwise help people suffering on the breadline or lower.

Impartiality comes to the fore only in limited 'public' arenas. As seen in Chapter 5, the humanist neutral state enjoins certain impartialities concerning employment opportunities, taxation and welfare. Impartiality applies to the private, when the public seeps into that private. When individuals let rooms, they should be impartial with regard to race, but not to ability to pay and keeping the music turned low. How far such impartiality should seep into personal lives is another moral and grey question. We embrace serpent windings in our reasoning when, for example, we feel morally at ease in dining so well with family and friends, while allowing so many, so very, very many, in other parts of the world – or even closer to home – to starve, suffer and die, uninvited to table. Think of political leaders who fly to world conferences on global poverty, conferences that just have to include banquets and feasts. Murder is morally wrong, but letting die – death at a distance? Arguably, morality, rather inconveniently, should know no geography; ethics, perhaps too conveniently, does. What we decide to embrace and stand up for need not be solely the moral life. Our reflection may lead us to support values other than moral.

The variety in life – our connections with others – can readily expose conflicts. In our tale of Mrs Jones, she may try the love affair on the side, betraying her husband's trust. Even if he never finds out, he may still be harmed, as argued earlier. It does not follow that avoidance of deception should always take the top priority. Love affairs may heighten life's affairs, even if also bringing regrets and remorse. In a murky and grey world, sometimes whatever one does may involve some wrong. Speaking the truth may hurt as much as deceiving. Again, on this, humanists happily have no 'the line', no scripture. It is case by case.

Because the excitements and sensualities of an illicit love affair benefit Mrs Jones at the expense of her family, it does not mean that they should be discounted. One's own life counts as do others. In a sense that many may recognize, Mrs Jones perhaps cannot go on the way she is. Something has to give; and pious comments about what is the morally right thing to do – what morality demands – may cast the possible actions and lives in different lights, but do not thereby determine what Mrs Jones, to live her life, flourish and relate well to others, should, or needs, to do. Judgement and decision enter. What sort of person is she to be?

There are – and are going to be – dilemmas and conflicts in many lives. What are the options available? How are they interpreted? What life can one live? What life can one live *with*?

We are now to confront questions of meaning, questions – as with those of morality – that should remind us of the inadequacies of reductionism, of all ultimately being answered using concepts from the physical sciences. Consider the Rosetta Stone: understanding the marks in terms of particles and forces would have missed their being inscriptions of Egyptian hieroglyphs and Ancient Greek, telling of a Ptolemaic decree.

In 1930, in conversation with Maurice Drury, Wittgenstein commented:

> I was walking about in Cambridge and passed a bookshop, and in the window were portraits of Russell, Freud and Einstein. A little further on, in a music shop, I saw portraits of Beethoven, Schubert and Chopin. Comparing these portraits I felt intensely the terrible degeneration that had come over the human spirit in the course of only a hundred years.

Humanism need not be committed to understanding everything by way of analysis. Humanists may speak of the human spirit. True, they do so without belief in spirits or an afterlife, yet they may still find meaning in life, as we are about to see.

7

Humanism: the quest for meaning

Once upon a time, in a far-away corner of the universe's glimmering effusion of countless solar systems, a star existed where wise creatures gave birth to knowledge. This was the most arrogant and the most dishonest minute of 'world history'; but it was only a minute. After nature had drawn breath a few times, the star froze, and the wise creatures had to die

Friedrich Nietzsche

We humanists know we shall cease to exist, yet we believe the world goes on. We build monuments, preserve libraries and save whales, when all will be lost. Vanity, all is vanity. Eternal life is the theists' answer; yet our lives need structure – development, shape – seemingly absent from eternity, from God. Arguably, the Nietzschean epigraph above puts us in our place – or, at the very least, makes us wonder about our place, about our perspective. And in this chapter, we encounter different perspectives, from within and without – perspectives detached from human life, even perspectives of humans losing themselves in books, plays or music.

Life is absurd. Within and without, life is absurd. Humanists and theists alike hold people morally responsible for their deeds, when we have little idea of what counts as 'responsible'. We speak of our *selves*, when we have no idea of what a self is. We fall in love, yearn and regret; we commit to futures with others, knowing full well that they, and we, change.

Absurdity here is incongruity. That fits well with the thought that what is distinctive of humanity is the ability to note wryly, to reflect, to pun, to laugh – incongruities indeed and not just in word.

Humanists often think – aspire, hope, trust – that, once they have exposed religions' absurdities, life's puzzles may be ironed out at least a little, that cooperation, reason and empathy may come to the rescue, not over the solar system's collapse and humanity's destruction, but over how our lives may be improved and how to view meaning and death. No doubt, many lives can go much better, but I doubt whether any of us can iron out life's creases and wrinkles – the conflicting perspectives, tensions and incongruities that we live by, and die by. I doubt the good sense of even wanting to do so.

Here, ironing is not the project. Uncovering absurdity, the chaos that yet keeps us going, is the project. I celebrate the chaos; others may not.

McTaggart's cat

McTaggart was a distinguished Cambridge philosopher who argued that the spatial-temporal world is but illusion, reality being an infinite number of loving souls. In cold winters, people who visited McTaggart's college rooms would be astonished to see his cat enjoying pride of position fireside front, while McTaggart shivered in a corner. 'Why ever do you give the cat the best position?' they would ask. 'Because,' replied McTaggart, 'that's the best it gets for a cat.'

We reflect on life. We reflect not just in philosophy classes, but at work, at dinner – and in the stillness of nights without sleep. Of course, sometimes we may feel the feline life is preferable; I remember the reflection well from my mother, when the going was tough. None the less most of us value being a person far more than being a cat. If the cat is too controversial an example, feel free to substitute down, to life as an ant, even a tree. Whatever evaluative disagreements, the humanist heart pumps awareness that only we humans can investigate and evaluate, aware that we do. Only we humans can explore skies so high and oceans so deep. Only we humans can marvel and wonder at fact and fancy. We discover mathematical truths and apply them to the world; we gaze at the world and send imaginations soaring. We demonstrate kindnesses, justice and beauty – and laugh at some jokes. There is far more to human life than feline. We value the more. (Chapter 9 looks further into this.)

Some human lives go well, some badly. Beware the mantra 'all lives are equally valuable' – something humanists can lapse into murmuring. 'Equal in what respect?' needs answering. Some suffer such great tragedies that they gain little from life. A few others are nasty, outstandingly deceitful and selfish. Our humanity, our empathy, pulls us towards equal concern for all; yet, stepping back, we may wonder why, and well wonder. Does the thuggish man merit as much concern as the female passer-by beaten up by aforementioned thug? Perhaps we should have no concern for the man, for *his* sake. Yet, investigate his upbringing – and, well, we may find ourselves understanding why he acted as he did. What chance had he? And yet ... Often we meet with no explanation at all from the world – and no remorse from him.

Humanists are tempted to think that 'deep down inside' each human is valuable. Arguably that is as much a faith picture as the Christians' – that Christ died for all sinners. Our humanity may push us along the path of hating the sin, but loving the sinner. Humanists probably also cannot help but reflect 'there but for the grace of God ...' Let us see how we muddle through about such matters – and others – without the call to the divine. We shall look first at our being held morally responsible for what we do and secondly at the nature of the self.

We award others, and ourselves, praise and blame, holding ourselves responsible, yet, if what we do is outside our control, praise and blame surely lack foundation. You are driving along, a wasp stings your hand; you lose control of the car and kill a pedestrian. That surely is not your fault; you are not *morally* to blame. Now, another scenario: you are driving along, rage mounting because of what your partner said; you lose control of the car and kill a pedestrian. You are to blame; you should have controlled your anger – yet could you? People are praised and blamed for their successes and failures. Successful hard workers differ from failed hard workers, yet the successful are lucky to possess their particular abilities, their nature and nurture. True, there exists a distinction between the industrious and lazy. Such character traits, though, result from a mixture of nature and nurture. People should not be praised or blamed for their luck or unluck; yet a matter of luck or unluck it is, that we are who we are. (For more, please see Rebekah's plight in Chapter 9.)

Theists have big perplexities with responsibility, whether they believe in predestination or free will, whether they emphasize God's grace or believe prayers help the lucky for whom they kneel and do pray. Humanists, with God deleted, still live within perplexities. Witness Richard Dawkins, outspoken defender of humanism: he seems to find room for human freedom in our being able to override behavioural tendencies from evolution. Our brains are 'separate and independent enough from our genes to rebel against them'. Putting to one side how brains can rebel: if, on the one hand, the rebellions stand outside causal explanations, then they are mysteries closed to scientific investigation – so, presumably not Dawkins's position. Let us, then, clasp the other hand: if, on this hand, our resisting certain tendencies does yield to causal explanations, why do those resistances count as free actions, whereas those explained genetically do not?

As said, we typically do see people as responsible for their actions, yet, by the little digging above, we have already struck some conceptual chaos usually hidden in everyday life. However, treating people as responsible agents, or at least *as if* responsible, is essential to our human relationships. If we did not, we should regard others as biological cogs and springs, or but blobs, to manipulate – as mere objects to use. And that is dangerous, for we cannot properly admire – befriend, resent – cogs and springs or biological blobs. Our treatment of people as people manifests humanism's emphasis on human beings' dignity, their autonomy. It sits incongruously with scientism, with explaining everything in terms of scientific laws, towards which some humanists are drawn. If a murderer is but a cog in a causal machine completely determined, then, as offender, he vanishes. Our moral indignation is no more appropriate than rebuking an earthquake.

When things are abnormal, we often do withdraw accolades of responsibility. The mentally ill avoid prison, but gain psychiatric units. The sane, we assume, have control over what they do; but have they any more ultimate control than the insane? At the very least, while we do regard the sane, others and ourselves, as to some degree autonomous, we also recognize the drives, the passions and emotions that can so overwhelm. All these are features that we share with the thuggish man mentioned above. He too is one of us – yet look what he did …

Maybe we retain some fellow feeling, despite Thug's thuggish ways. If, on the one hand, he was battered by passions outside his control, perhaps we can grasp how we could be too. If, on the other hand, he acted deliberately, freely, well, why then do we care about him, concerned for his life? Maybe we care because, optimistically, we think – whatever he does and says – goodness lurks somewhere within. Maybe we care because, pessimistically, we think that – whatever we do and say – we could have been as bad as he is. Probably, we are simply baffled, groping at the thought that he did not have to grow up to be as he is: there must have been overwhelming harms in his upbringing, bad crowds surrounding him, no good models to emulate.

And those reflections cast us into our second conundrum: just who is he? Or, in the first person, what is this 'I' – these 'I's – that concern and trouble us so much?

Theists speak of life after death – meaning it literally and already incongruously. Humanists smile smugly at such a silly idea. Yet, in one way we all, humanists included, live with similar silliness, or, at least, perplexity. Let us approach this via another typical humanist position, namely, the rejection of afterlife living.

Some theists believe in bodily resurrection. They are, of course, suitably baffled by the state and age of bodies so resurrected. The atoms constituting our bodies disperse over the years, even becoming constituents of a mish-mash of other humans. 'Of course, God can work all that out.' Really … ? Some theists believe we are immaterial, immortal souls, souls that make us the distinctive individual humans that we are. Such disembodied, immaterial beings lack appeal to humanists. Humanists value human beings with bodies, in contrast to many theists, ever keen to escape the body, believing it even corrupt and evil, many of its lusts maybe the work of the devil.

Humanists are baffled over how a disembodied existence could even be *personal* survival. First, there exist bewildering questions concerning what a soul is. Secondly, what separates one soul from another? Thirdly, what makes *me* identical with this disembodied soul rather than that? Perhaps our continuing personal existence is not continuation of the same immaterial soul, but a continuity and connectedness of psychological states, through memory, beliefs and attitudes. So long as, through time, there are overlapping psychological processes – my memories and thoughts – maybe I thereby persist, and could even continue forever. Once disembodied, though, it is unclear whether we can have experiences of sight, touch and so forth. Further, all we should be able to do, it seems, is to think, mull and muse. I vaguely recall Descartes hypothesizing that the immortal life would be an intellectual life of reflection on morality and mathematics, on virtue and triangles. It lacks some appeal.

Afterlife living is baffling, yet, here on earth, we live deep puzzles, of what makes someone the same person through time. This is no place to observe the fine philosophical jousting. We may note, though, that Hume sent out a search party for the self. He looked within himself and could find no self – just memories, thoughts and perceptions. Probably that is the wrong way of setting about the problem, but no other way has yet yielded convincing answers. There is the psychological continuity answer just mentioned, but is that convincing? Suppose you are to be tortured tomorrow, yet just before the torture you will have your memories and thoughts wiped out, a forced amnesia. You would still experience the torturing pain, even though no longer knowing who you are.

Perhaps being you is more a matter of your body continuing rather than the psychology; yet that approach also has problems. After all, it looks as if you can make sense of all your body's atoms being changed, yet you remain you; it looks as if you can make sense of bodily exchanges. Perhaps being you is a matter of either/or, either the psychological or the bodily continuity – yet that can also baffle.

Humanists, as do we all, make frequent use of a concept – the self, 'I', 'me' – which is arguably as obscure as the concept of God, as just noted. There is one essential difference. None of us can make sense of our living without using the 'I' concept. Millions of people live their lives perfectly well without the godly.

We have raised puzzles concerning responsibility and self. The puzzles impinge upon us in many ways – in mind and body ways. We love the person for her charm, her intellect – the curve of his lips, the coquettishness of her step – yet must that love, to be true, remain, even when the charm, the intellect, the curves and the coquettish have vanished? Athletes seek fairness in sport. They want to see what runners can truly achieve by themselves. So, performance-enhancing drugs are banned; yet not performance-enhancing training.

We all muddle through, often pretending there is clarity, when in fact there is chaos, cloaked chaos.

The mouse

Within our lives – in our everyday living – we often find things highly important. Yet step outside and our lives are utterly insignificant. 'Only God can make them significant' – yet, God is precisely what humanism lacks.

A mouse's life, as Thomas Nagel argues, is not absurd; a human life is. A mouse's life contains no incongruity; a human's does. The mouse scurries about, satisfying desires, never stepping outside her life, never reflecting on the significance of her scurry. We, humans, though, can cast ourselves outside all life, taking up perspectives from another star, from the universe's edge, or from nowhere at all. From such ultimate perspectives, human life in total is as of nothing, as the Nietzschean epigraph implies – and all the more so is our own particular life. Is it not utterly ridiculous that things should matter so much to us, when from outside they matter not at all? Think how we humans scurry, how some things strike us as so important – whether the hairstyle is quite right, the career going well, whether the late arrival was a slight, and as for that first grey hair ... Yet all are insignificant – under the aspect of eternity.

Such reflections – reflections of a perspectival clash – may cause despair, making our lives appear meaningless; but we could reflect further that, as things do not matter from the outside, it does not matter that they do not matter. And so, we should get on with life, as does Miss Mouse. We may even question whether there is the described incongruity between our viewpoint within our lives and the detached outer viewpoint 'from the universe' or 'from nowhere': no sense can be made of mattering from a viewpoint that is really no viewpoint at all. And yet ...

Sometimes the suggestion is that we are alone in a universe that is indifferent to us. But that thought – of the uncaring universe – is a mistaken thought. The universe is not the sort of thing that is either indifferent or caring. Other people can be indifferent to me; the universe cannot. And yet ...

We sometimes worry about our lives ultimately not mattering, given that we are such tiny specks in a universe so vast. If the problem – a problem of size mattering – is that we are so spatially small, well, conceive us big; expand us spatially to fill the universe. If the problem is our temporal teeniness; expand us that way too. Let us become the whole of the universe, in space, in time. Does that therefore help to make us ultimately matter? The answer is 'no'. Whatever features we may propose to make us ultimately matter, we may always ask why possession of those features matters.

Humanism brings us back down to earth. Meanings are simply given within our lives, and to our lives through others. That is part of what matters. What matters is also, for example, getting at the truth – getting at the truth, for example, of what matters. And yet ...

'If my life ends with death, then my doings have been without point.' The sorrowful sigh is often heard; and in bleakness, in shadows of night's stillness, it moves many.

Of course, the sigh expresses no truth. My doings may have point within my life and also in affecting others. Many people find point through children, grandchildren, great-grandchildren, pets and projects – being part of a bigger enterprise: the arts club, the college, the humanitarian cause, even, sadly, the gang that terrorizes neighbours. People sometimes insist that life requires point through things external to that life; and then, they insist, those things too require point. 'The point of A is B,' we may say. 'Ah,' they shake their heads, 'but what is the point of B?' 'C,' we reply. 'Not good enough,' they say, 'for what is the point of C?' If, for something to be meaningful, it must have point, and if points must always be external, also possessing point, then we shall be forever inconsolable. But that is only because we have set ourselves a logically impossible demand. As it is logically impossible, we should come to see that there is nothing actual or possible to be concerned about. And yet ...

'If my life is eternal, then all is well.' That is the theistic hope. But, if we may sensibly ask the point of this or that, we may also ask, 'What is the point of eternal life?' If 'to the glory of God' is the response, then the question again arises. What is the point of glorifying God? We should not, by the way, settle for the thought that things are fine, if we are part of some unknown divine plan. Whether things are fine or not depends on the plan. Do grouse have meaningful lives because they are part of a greater plan, a plan that reaches its climax on the glorious twelfth, when they are shot? Whatever is said along the lines of eternity and God, if our present life is a riddle, then so is the eternal and God.

One mistake that gives rise to the disquiet about meaning is that we can too readily and sharply divide our activities into means and ends, between the doings and points of those doings. We then run the danger of valuing only the points, the ends. Indeed, we run the danger of closing our eyes to how the badness of the means deployed may outweigh the advantages of the ends sought. Reflect, for example, on the constant improvements going on to roads and offices and homes in typical towns – to improve the quality of life. Yet the continuing screeches and drillings and other disruptions, through the improvements' workings, diminish the desired quality.

A life of immediately realizing all ends would be no life at all. If everything that you sought, you simply secured at the press of a button; well, what then? Achieving a goal may be valuable, but that usually involves *not* suddenly securing the goal, but being entangled in all the activities on the way. Travelling has point – not merely for its point. There is also value in activities that have no point at all, in play, in games, for example.

Death, in fact, helps living and the living. Without death, we may find it difficult to structure a life. Apart from the thought, often expressed, that an immortal life would be tedious, with such immortality we should not recognize ourselves. The courage to rescue someone in danger, the concern for our flourishing and others' – the need to get up in the morning – all these would, at the very least, undergo radical changes. These remarks do not, of course, mean that much longer lives would not often be better. Of course, they could be worse. Many of us, though, would like to know how things turn out; and that is certainly one thing, it seems, that we shall never know. We are trapped within humanity's horizons.

We are trapped within humanity's horizons, yet we seek to step outside. 'What if in reality my whole life has been wrong?' That question, asked by Tolstoy's Ivan Illyich, may make us uneasy. As we grow older, we may become ashamed of our past: we may reflect on wasted years, spot mistaken turnings, recognizing occasions when we failed to stand up for what we believed. Our lives, as wholes, may be judged to be seriously wrong compared with standards once embraced or embraced now. We may even step outside our lives, wondering whether our current standards – our desires, aspirations, lives – are themselves all wrong. Some then shudder, repent and hope for God's grace.

Humanism rejects the eternal judge, but perhaps sense may be made of our lives having been all wrong, from an outside perspective, even without judgers. After all, we had some grip on this idea – but how well did it fare? – when comparing the feline with the human and when noting how some lives go better than others.

Some of us cannot resist seeking the objective viewpoint, a viewpoint undistorted by preferences and position. We achieve this a little. There are degrees and degrees of local distortion. Just think of the head spinning after too much partying, of stepping outside current woes, in order to see the bigger picture or picture unspun. But once we push on further, we fall into obscurities, of wanting, maybe, to choose what sort of people to be. Sophocles, indeed, speculated that the happiest are those not to have been born. The thought sends minds spinning. What sense can even be made of such detached reflections?

Of course, humanists do live lives, believing that there are worldly truths, independent of humanity and ungrounded in God, even though humans may struggle to uncover them. Perhaps we should also accept that some truths concern what is good and bad, independent of human judgement and nature. Yet how is that possible? Humanists tend to believe that, as values lack divine source, humanity must, in some way, be the source. There is, though, between God and humanity, a third option. Well, let us try ...

What is the property of being good? Utilitarians, as we saw, answer in terms of being happy. Other answers are that good states are just those that bring forth human approval. Such answers, argued G. E. Moore, commit the naturalistic fallacy, akin to the fallacy, seen in Chapter 3, of identifying goodness with God's commands. Quite what is fallacious about the fallacy is moot; but, at heart, take any proposal for what constitutes being good: we may then ask whether what is proposed is indeed good. This question, though, does not amount to asking whether, say, increasing happiness is increasing happiness. So, the property of being good differs from the property of

'YOU WANT TO LIVE "ACCORDING TO NATURE"?'

Friedrich Nietzsche (1844–1900) famously announced that God is dead. Søren Kierkegaard (1813–1855) took a leap of faith into God. Yet they are both now considered existentialists, emphasizing how human beings need to choose what to be and do, as later did Sartre. Humanists also emphasize choice, but arguably have a more realistic understanding. Humanists recognize that we are limited by features common to humanity; and some of the features are valuable, notably our fellow feeling.

We need to be wary of talk of nature and how we should live 'according to nature'. Such talk is fraudulent, says Nietzsche. 'Think of a being such as nature is, prodigal beyond measure, without aims or intentions, indifferent beyond measure, without mercy or justice, at once fruitful and barren and uncertain; think of indifference itself as a power – how *could* you live according to such indifference? To live – is that not precisely wanting to be other than this nature?'

I have heard it said that Nietzsche's thoughts were so disturbing, they sent him mad. Yes, he did go mad – but from syphilis.

increasing happiness. In rebuttal, some, as seen, point out that it is a substantial question whether water is H_2O, yet none the less water is just that. With goodness, though, the position is different: there seems no way of justifiably settling on a proposed naturalistic answer as correct. This perhaps is why Moore insisted that goodness could not be a natural, or indeed a godly, property or a complex of such.

For many humanists, moral properties are queer, if they are not natural, causal and available to scientific investigation, yet, we should remember, mathematical objects are, then, also queer. Numbers are not 'in nature'; numbers lack causal powers – but we are not driven to God because we lack physical analyses of numbers. So, too, perhaps we should be relaxed about moral properties. Further, moral properties should not be causal. That something is good may show us what we morally ought to do, yet it does not, of course, cause us to do it.

There remains the question of which items and activities have any given moral or other evaluative property. As noted earlier, human beings in the main agree on some – and argue about others. Although moral goodness and rightness are not mere matters of how people feel or think, were human beings or similar not to exist, arguably there would be no actions that were right or wrong. There could still exist some items of value and some more valuable than others: for example, consciousness may have its own value – and a sunset over the ocean may be more beautiful than space with a few rocks. Those examples manifest the idea that some things, unconnected with humans, are intrinsically good, though maybe not morally so. There may well be something radically odd about the idea. Humanists often feel uneasy, seeing it as sliding towards a creator-designer. But a universe with items of independent value is no more likely to have a creator-designer than a universe with no items of value at all.

Some seek foundations of morality. Dawkins, for example, claims to provide good Darwinian reasons for individuals to be 'moral' towards each other, yet, as already noted, he also encourages us to rebel against certain genetically grounded tendencies. So, contrary to appearance, he has given no explanation of why we morally should behave one way rather than another, rebel in some cases, yet not others. More generally, just because there may be scientific explanations of the source, or evolution, of our behaviour they would not thereby be explanations of the nature of moral values. There is an explanation of how we are able to see items around us, but that does not explain which items there are to be seen.

Even when we all agree on moral matters, reflective people may worry: what justifies us in thinking that killing that girl is morally wrong? 'Obviously, it is. She's not harming any one.'

'But why does that show that *objectively* it is wrong?' Once a foundational answer is provided, we may seek a foundation for that foundation. And so on. Yet, recalling Chapter 2, explanations have to come to an end. To follow a line of Moore, whatever sceptical arguments may be brought against our belief that killing the innocent is morally wrong, we are more certain that the killing is morally wrong than that the argument is sound. Consider another example: the power of deduction. From 'All men are mortal' and 'Socrates is a man', it follows that 'Socrates is mortal'. The argument is valid – but can we justify that validity? We cannot, without using valid arguments and raising the question again. So, too, with morality, one has to stop somewhere. Torturing an innocent child for the sheer fun of it is morally wrong. Full stop.

Muddling through

Humanists accuse godly believers of illusions, yet, as seen above, we all live lives with some illusions, myths and conflicting perspectives. We face moral and ethical dilemmas; we juggle incommensurable factors. We appeal to the natural, to rights and duties and virtues and self-interest and 'judgement' – though there are often no rules for judging. We may live as if there is always 'the right answer', telling us which one of various alternatives we morally must do; but often such an answer is lacking.

When morally juggling, we often insist, 'It is a matter of judgement, of balance.' We want to distinguish our deliberations from flicks of the wrist or throws of the dice. Yet, but for the anguishing and ritual of reasoning, we may question whether a morally relevant difference exists. For a related example, turn to the law, to courts, to courts of appeal, to the House of Lords, to the American Supreme Court. Final decisions there hang on majority votes with equally expert judges often delivering opposing verdicts. Had, indeed, different judges sat, had different judges been appointed, results would have been different. On such factors hangs whether defendants are deemed fraudsters, rapists or war criminals. 'But are the judgements right? Were they really fraudsters, rapists or whatever?' We may ask such questions, bewitched by the desire for the black or white, when right answers often involve 'to some degree' and 'in some respects'. We could cite hundreds of examples, from voting procedures to taxation to school examinations, where fairness and reasonableness have to be invoked, yet where what counts as fair and reasonable can be moveable posts or areas of greyness.

Humanism tells us that it is our own individual responsibility to do the best that we can, despite those flaws and fancies. And, while we may turn to others for forgiveness when we have wronged them, they cannot forgive us for what we have done to ourselves, to our own life, to how we have lived. Here the humanist resource just is oneself. 'What can I live with?'

Some take their lives seriously; some lives are carefree. Either way, there is something that we are standing for. Many of us, at times, in one way or another, wonder how we should fill our life, instead of just letting ourselves be swept along. Wittgenstein wrote: 'How small a thought it takes to fill a whole life.' This may be read as a sigh of joy – or of despair. How impressed we should be by the power of a small idea? – or how depressed that a triviality could keep us so satisfied?

Some humanists appeal to reason to sort out how best to live, yet reason itself generates paradoxical positions. In 'prisoner's dilemma' cases, rational things to do by self-interested individuals seem guaranteed not to give best outcomes for those self-interested individuals. Humanists, as we have seen, also turn to human nature, to fellow feeling; yet while there is much that is

splendid and bright in human nature – and nature more widely
– we all know too well of corruption and decay. As William
Blake reflects:

O Rose, thou art sick!
The invisible worm
That flies in the night,
In the howling storm,

Has found out thy bed
Of crimson joy:
And his dark secret love
Does thy life destroy.

There are sinister features in humanity – which sometimes bubble
forth, sometimes rest dormant – as well as the inspiring features
of dignity. There are passions that we embrace – and passions that
we cast asunder and reject.

As we make choices in life, we grow into individuals with
character – with history, style, attitude and approach to life. With
no God to instruct us – and desirous of none – we may turn to
models: either/or, either this way of life or that. Kierkegaard presented the choice between the aesthetic, moral (termed 'ethical'
by Kierkegaard) and religious; that is, between the sensual, our
moral duty, and religious faith, the latter requiring a leap. Many of
us zigzag between the first two. The biblical Abraham remained
true to the third, his religious leap, when prepared to sacrifice his
son – surely not a duty that morality would impose.

The struggle between the sensual and morality is worth pursuing. The struggle is ubiquitous, significant and can dominate
lives. Because it is all these things, it frequently features in the
arts. Look at *Don Giovanni* – Mozart's opera – not least because
opera itself manifests absurdity, with audiences rapt as singers sing
through lives.

'IN THE LONG RUN, WE ARE ALL DEAD'

So said John Maynard Keynes (1883–1946), the great economist, a humanist, one only too well aware of life's conflicts, yet who handled them magnificently. Keynes helped others, being exceptionally generous to his friends, yet also, through his economic policies, aiming to improve the welfare of all. Religion was hocus-pocus; conventional sexual morality was ignored. Yet, despite his wayward reputation – he had many affairs with men, then married a successful Russian ballerina – he became an establishment figure, his funeral service being held in Westminster Abbey, London.

Keynes encouraged the anguished philosopher, Wittgenstein, as well as the humanist Frank Ramsey, whom we meet at the end of this chapter. Keynes was part of the Bloomsbury Group, supported the arts, and enjoyed the odd day pig farming. His was a flourishing life. He was often charged with changing his mind. Humanists welcome mind-changes, being untied to dogmas.

By the way, Keynes's response to the mind-changing charge was, 'When the facts change, I change my mind. What do you do, sir?'

The Don lives only for sexual conquest, driven solely by desire. He slays and betrays – to achieve seduction after seduction, gathering, devouring and discarding. Morality lacks power over him. The Don receives various staged representations. Metaphorically, he is an irrepressible cosmic principle, sometimes an obsessive, a neurotic, even sometimes a latent homosexual. Some portray him as a seeker after an ideal.

The Don seduces every woman; the opera seduces many. It highlights conflicts within. Maybe the Don just is all primitive desire – not even a person – contrasting with the opera's women, who are possessed of genuine individuality and identity. The Don is perhaps the exuberance of human life, unconstrained: humans are sometimes defiant against well-entrenched, well-grounded conventions, and often against conventions that seem nothing but conventions. We humans often prize lack of restraint. Yet we also prize boundaries, individuality, love for other individuals, fairness, respect – even some conventional rules by way of etiquette and 'the done thing'.

A dichotomy here is between the Apollonian and Dionysian. On the one hand, the image of Apollo signifies a rational world of limits, of distinct objects, of rules – a clenched fist in control. The image gives rise to aesthetic ideas of the simple, beautiful, precise and lucid. Plato offered the image of love, our rising to love the form of beauty itself. We humans may aspire to such ideals. On the other hand, the Dionysian is intoxication, drunkenness, where boundaries become blurred, through ecstasy and frenzy. The Dionysian breaks down barriers. Palms are open, welcoming, yielding. It may draw us into worlds of universal harmony. It can also be a dangerous brew: with all barriers down, anything goes, and lusts may know no limits.

The struggle between control and frenzy, and yet their ultimate coexistence, is part of many human lives. Consider Thomas Mann's *Death in Venice*, be it the novella, Visconti film or Britten opera. There, Gustav von Aschenbach, the personification of the Apollonian, the disciplined rational writer, admirer of beauty and form, is struck by the beauty of the mysterious teenage boy, Tadzio, a beauty of purity. The story tells of Aschenbach becoming swept along by the sensual – the senses leading to passion – with Aschenbach eventually seeming degraded, degraded by an old man's erotic love for a youth; yet maybe he captured a sense of something valuable and previously unknown. Interpretations can hang in the air, 'the black or the white' banished.

Few of us think or live, or even want to think or live, in terms of such explicit categories, itself an Apollonian enterprise; yet in human lives we recognize so easily the conflicts between discipline and frenzy, control and succumbing, order and chaos, dominance and submission – straight lines and tangles. Theists see themselves as living lives according to God's will, whereas we humanists have only stories, plays and music to represent lives, to inspire us. Yet, the theists row with us in life's same boat. Their godly ways, in reality, are viewed in the light of stories, plays and music – scriptures and rituals – though, it is true, theists think that they see a divine imprimatur. They ignore the fact that they have no means of determining the fake from the true.

Whether fake or true, some scriptural tales hold a continuing fascination for both believers and non-believers. The tales intermingle with new ways of seeing, ways generated by non-believing psychoanalysis, philosophy and art, music and stage. An example is Richard Strauss's *Salome*, the music and performances driving an intense sexuality, religious mystery, decadence and horror – with the ambiguity of family relationships, the clash of freedom and obsession, the presence of individuals who even here on earth can do no other.

For theists, earthly life offers eternal heaven – some Keynesian hocus-pocus. For humanists, earthly life is all we have. And it can offer both too much and yet too little. Perhaps one would like to try out the life of the artist, yet also of the scientist; of the unworldly, yet also the worldly; of the loyal family man or woman, yet also the Casanova or courtesan; of the passive, yet also the active. We may be tempted by a life of solitude, yet also one filled with friends; of a life alone by the sea and stars, yet also a gregarious city life, with theatres and dinners. Lifestyles rule out others. The whole life of conformity rules out the life of variety. Greyness cuts out rainbows. Simplicity denies complexity.

Losing the self

What does give value to life? There are achievements. There are friendships. There are the immersions within tangles of moon-lit discussions, of feeling at one with others, of incongruities in humour, of the cold drink of water on a hot afternoon – or simply fingertips touching. There are experiences and curiosities: a shadow flickering, the familiarity of a beloved aria, a face in the clouds; the word spins of a poetess, the averted eyes, the pun in a comedy sketch, the sense of 'life on the edge' when overcome by jealousy. Yet, with any of these, we may hear the nagging voice, 'But are they really meaningful?'

Curiously, although we make much use of the self – of 'I' – of our personal existence, and our worry about death, things often go best when we have *lost our selves* or are near to so doing. Whatever you enjoy – be it watching thrillers, reading novels, theatre-going, listening to music, studying, playing the piano, even playing baseball – when you look back, you discover that you were lost in the story, the movement, the emotions, the sounds, the thoughts, the competition. When the last page is turned, or the credits roll or the applause thunders, you are brought up sharp, brought back to the world. This is most odd; it may even tempt us now to think that there is a lot to be said for the life of McTaggart's cat, even for the Sophoclean reflection that the happiest are those never to have been born – for then one's self is truly lost. Yet we know that here lies mystery, that things are not as simple as that. In some way, we were aware of enjoying the novel, the play, the music – and yet, in another way, we did not exist, save in as far as we were distracted by some whispering or by sensations of over-heating. Such mysteries provide a pull towards the mystics, the spiritual, of losing oneself in … well, what? Fill in the gap.

And so, too, we often lose ourselves in our everyday lives, everyday lives without absurdity. Yet, let us step back and reflect on those lives. Then absurdities fill our view, the incongruities and tensions. And one thing humanists are prepared to do is give a wry smile at those absurdities – and pity the cat and the mouse. They know of no absurdity. They know of no smiles.

★   ★   ★

Allow F. P. Ramsey, a humanist big in body, yet short in lifespan – a brilliant mathematician, economist and philosopher, yet also one who delighted in music, mountain-climbing and romance – to bring us back to humanist good sense:

> I don't feel the least humble before the vastness of the heavens. The stars may be large, but they cannot think or love; and these are qualities which impress me far more than size does. I take no credit for weighing nearly seventeen stone. My picture of the world is drawn in perspective, and not to scale. The foreground is occupied by human beings and the stars are all as small as threepenny bits ... I apply my perspective not merely to space but also to time. In time the world will cool and everything will die; but that is a long time off still, and its present value at compound discount is almost nothing. Nor is the present less valuable because the future will be blank. Humanity, which fills the foreground of my picture, I find interesting and on the whole admirable.

That is indeed good sense from Ramsey, yet it is good sense from the privileged perspective of a much-admired young Cambridge don in 1925, a don with a feeling for humanity and, seemingly, a great future ahead. He died five years later. With life's uncertainty in mind, the next two chapters attend to some global realities, including extinction, that humanists – all of us – must face.

8

Pan-disasters, pan-deceptions and pandemonium

No one is safe until everyone is safe.

Global mantra

Dinosaurs and other 'saurs' – mosasaurs, ichthyosaurs, pterosaurs – flourished for many an age, yet worldwide disaster, a pan-disaster, eventually befell. Those prehistoric reptilians came to a sticky end circa 65 million years ago. The disaster of extinction, if disaster it be, has not, of course, happened to human beings – yet. There have, though, been many disasters for human beings; and now dangers of possible pandemics are ever present – as are portentous climate changes, suggestive of a perilous future.

Humanity has been lucky with the Covid-19 pandemic – so far – that is, at the time of writing in 2022. Billions of human beings have survived, largely unscathed. It has, though, been tragic for millions; it has caused a great many to suffer and has led to the premature deaths of some millions of those millions. Things could have been worse. The virus could have been one that spread more easily, against which no vaccine would be effective and for which there would be no treatment to prevent fatalities.

Climate change, as noted, is also presented as a significant threat to humanity – another potential pan-disaster. No doubt global warming is taking place; no doubt, minimally, it will disrupt the lives of millions. The danger, however great it be, is mainly to future generations, to generations after generations, unless – it is currently argued – certain radical changes are made in today's living. How far should we look into the future? Who can make reasonable judgements about how things will turn out hundreds of years hence, whatever changes we do or do not make now? As quipped, the Second Law of Thermodynamics will get us in the end, should nothing else do so first – and that nothing else will do so first is amazingly unlikely.

Coping with Covid-19 delivered severe impositions on lives; handling climate change dangers is generating other impositions. This chapter uses the pandemic to illustrate certain challenges to humanist values – challenges that also arise because of climate change – and then turns to climate change's distinctive puzzle.

Pandemic

The 'humanity has been lucky' mantra related to the survival of human beings through the pandemic – but has humanity been lucky by way of the survival of humanism's values? Those values, as seen in previous chapters, include respect for people's freedom, dignity and welfare, and commitments to compassion, fairness and fellow feeling. Intermeshed is the need for honesty, trust and trustworthiness. Many religions promote adherence to those values, but only in as far as they harmonize with believers' interpretations of divine commands. We should also remind ourselves that some human beings value what should be disvalued: a disregard for the interests of others, be it through greed, dishonesty or remaining silent when one should speak out. All of us (perhaps an odd exception exists) at times and to varying degrees, with a variety of enthusiasms and excuses, manifest those disvalues.

The Covid-19 pandemic has drawn immediate attention to both values and disvalues. Some people, some governments, have become more aware of the value of community, of fellow feeling, of helping those who have suffered from the virus or from attempted controls of the virus. Medical staff and many others have gone 'beyond the call of duty'; they have been heroic. Neighbourliness has come to the fore. Well-off helpers in Britain, when supplying essentials to the lockdown isolated, have been surprised and shocked by the poverty so close, encountering for the first time people who lacked cooking facilities and hot water.

Not all have manifested 'fellow feeling'. A few companies – that is, corporate directors – have taken advantage of the urgency for medical supplies; some individuals have made fraudulent claims for financial assistance. Certain people have abused the public by spreading 'fake news' via social media of how lockdown measures were but cunning steps towards totalitarianism, or how the Covid-19 story was but a corporately inspired ruse to expand health-related sales or control our minds through vaccinations. Certain politicians have corrupted the public's understanding by deeming Covid-19 'Chinese', leading to hatred directed against Chinese and other Asian communities. A curious mismatch existed between the British government's condemnation of the Chinese authority's apparent concealment of the viral source and the government's own reluctance to come clean about its pandemic inadequacies and dubieties.

Mixed into all this have been conflicting attitudes towards science. The swift vaccine developments have typically been praised, but the epidemiological researches leading to various restrictions on everyday life have been much condemned by some, yet valued by others. The source of Covid-19 has usually been accepted as zoonotic – transmitted from non-human animals to humans – but that has been doubted by those who focus on China's Wuhan Institute of Virology as the possible source, pointing to the dangers of scientific research.

These conflicts and deceits have not exactly been helpful in generating trust in leaderships, be they political, corporate or scientific. Eyes have, though, been opened to how interconnected we are across the globe; of course, at some level we already knew that. Eyes have been opened to many things that, again at some level, we already knew: the existence of vast inequalities within countries, the vast inequalities between countries – and regarding the UK, the underfunding of social care and health services, the extent of homelessness and so forth. For some, there has grown a feeling of solidarity within a nation and an increasing awareness of solidarity needed between nations.

Pandemonium

'There have been as many plagues as wars in history', wrote Albert Camus, 'yet always plagues and wars take people equally by surprise.' The Covid-19 surprise – a surprise despite the pandemic potential of 2002–2003 SARS, 2012 MERS and 2014 Ebola; despite scientific recommendations for pandemic readiness 'just in case' – led to pandemonium for liberal democracies. Humanism supports liberal democracies – recall John Stuart Mill's Liberty Principle (Chapter 5) – and liberal democracies have been unsettled by challenges to beloved values of freedom and autonomy through mandatory lockdowns, vaccination requirements and restrictions on personal relationships. There has been disorder, confusion, bedlam about what is best to do.

Expectations of comfortable lives have been shattered for many – and not just expectations. Lockdowns led certain individuals into psychological crisis; some suffered domestic abuse; for others, medical conditions worsened. More generally, a greater awareness of death and human fragility has come to the fore. Some good just possibly may result. The awareness may encourage a sense of humility and reflection on how lucky in life many of us have been. It may help the well-off to feel for those millions who have no prospect of comfortable lives – whose lives have daily been on the edge. My 'just possibly' is likely, though, to be wildly optimistic, for people can be pretty adept at putting the sufferings of others to the back of their minds. To quote Joseph Roth, the Austrian novelist, 'Once the emergency becomes protracted, helping hands return to pockets.'

Religions undergo the usual unsettlings when disasters occur: how are they to square the latest ones with God's omnipotence and omnibenevolence? Humanists at least lack that puzzle, but they face disruption of their own values. Consider the introduction of rigid lockdowns. Most United Kingdom citizens supported the introduction; some were fiercely opposed. It would be astonishing if all humanists were on the same side. The problem is, as ever, how to deal with competing values. Thomas Hobbes, in the seventeenth century, ever conscious of the then plagues and civil wars, summed it up thus:

> For in a way beset with those that contend on one side for too great Liberty, and on the other side for too much Authority, 'tis hard to passe between the points of both unwounded.

Even in the good times, we face the problem of how to 'passe unwounded': the pandemic highlighted it for nearly everyone – with the varying demands, from full lockdowns to 'social' (surely, physical) distancing to face coverings and so forth. The conflict was between biosecurity for the population and respect for people to live lives as they choose. Let us reflect upon two aspects of this – the religious and the evidential – before turning to the fundamental humanist value of freedom or liberty.

With regard to religious belief determining pandemic responses, humanists have easy dismissal. For that matter, many sincere religious believers dismissed certain religious arguments as outlandish. Some evangelical Christians in the United States, for example, argued that wearing face coverings constituted an offence to God. Humanists, obviously, have no truck with that, yet things are not quite that simple; after all, humanists typically support religious freedoms and, without being outlandish, many religious believers value worship as an essential community activity. The standard humanist response would have to be that in emergencies religious freedoms must be overriden for protection of the population's welfare – assuming that, at least as precautions, lockdowns were required. After all, illness and death do not exactly promote people's liberty or future opportunities to worship.

The humanist stance would oppose the April 2021 Hindu Kumbh Mela festival in Haridwar, where millions of devotees dipped in the holy Ganges, cleansing themselves of sins and bringing salvation, yet aiding the viral spread, suffering and death. The devotees presumably would argue that the cleansing was more important than viral control; cleansing offers eternal benefit. In Britain, certain ultra-Orthodox Jews held large wedding celebrations as fundamental to their flourishing; again, humanists typically would need to oppose. Of course, many non-believers promoted their own priorities – for large attendances at football matches, lively and crowded bars or nightclub raves – even though with risks of subsequent widespread viral transmission, endangering the common welfare.

The dissent over face coverings may be contrasted with certain dissents over religious coverings – the veil. The latter has been on the political agenda because of conservative Islamic adherents insisting that Muslim women's faces must be covered when in public, be it via the niqab or burqa. For those Muslims, it hugely matters. For the French Republic, it hugely matters – but leading to prohibition. There, religious veils are perceived as undermining the neutral public arena, essential for a liberal secular democracy, for France's *Laïcité*; coverings to reduce viral transmission lack that undermining.

Most humanists in Britain reject both the Islamic importance given to the attire and the danger, as the French government sees it, of public secular space being eroded. Valuing free expression,

British humanists have no problem with religious attire in public, assuming freely worn. The French and British responses show how humanists' liberal secular values can be so differently applied. Let us reflect a little further.

Suppose increasing numbers of people in Britain become committed to a conservative interpretation of Islam, creating pressure on some Muslim women to be veiled; suppose that leads to more and more women, Muslim or no, experiencing unease if not covered – and hence they feel compelled minimally to dress more 'modestly', particularly in areas where conservative Islamic belief is dominant. How far does that need to go before the British humanists' respect for religious freedom of dress gives way to the French approach? Yes, humanists value free expression even of ways of living that humanists do not value – but only so far. Freedom receives no blanket humanist support, as we shall further see regarding pandemic controls.

Religion apart, there have been straightforward empirical disagreements over Covid-19 restrictions. Lockdowns have led to sufferings and deaths. There have been certain increases in domestic violence, mental illness and worsening of some non-Covid illnesses. Some have wrongly concluded that things would have been better overall without lockdowns. True, things would have been better without lockdowns, but we can be certain of that only if there were no pandemic. There were no good reasons to believe that things would have been better without lockdowns yet with the pandemic raging. I am reminded of the Lazy Argument examined by ancient Greek philosophers: an ill person argues that either he is going to get better or not – if he is going to get better, there is no need to trouble doctors; if he is not going to get better, it is pointless to trouble doctors. Here is a Covid-19 version: either the virus will spread or not – if it will spread, why suffer lockdowns in addition? If it will not spread, lockdowns are unnecessary. Either way, lockdowns are unnecessary.

No one, as far as I know, has shown that the pandemic without restrictions would have led to considerable fewer deaths and less suffering than the pandemic with the restrictions. Of course, what it was reasonable to do at the time when the pandemic threatened – given the severity and credibility of the danger – may differ from what it would have been reasonable to do had more been known. The humanist stance respects the evidence regarding risk and degree of danger, and that requires respecting Keynes's dictum, met earlier, 'When the facts change, I change my mind. What do you do, sir?'

Lovers of liberty often have knee-jerk reactions when governments intrude into personal lives. The Great Barrington Declaration of October 2020, supported by a minority of medical and scientific experts, though some distinguished, argued that instead of lockdowns there should have been 'focused protection': the vulnerable receive protection, while others go about their lives normally. How 'focused protection' could be achieved in Great Britain received little more than silence. Millions of people live in multi-generational and crowded households. Many individuals from those households, some elderly, some vulnerable, some young, were required for essential public services – they were hospital staff, shelf-stackers, postal workers, bus drivers, street cleaners … – leading to likely Covid contact unless severe restrictions were in place. Further, were it to have been practically possible to separate out the vulnerable, it would align with Foucault's observation of how the leper gave rise to 'rituals of exclusion'. Such rituals are hardly freedom loving.

'Set the people free'

Faced with lockdowns or lesser restrictions, some simply trumpeted 'liberty'. While the trumpet may be appropriate on marchers' placards, it is of negligible practical use, though, yes, some declare liberty as manifestly of top priority. Even if empirical calculations for lockdowns show them necessary and right for society's protection overall, paradoxically they are wrong. Even if more deaths or sufferings would have occurred without lock-downs, that is a pity but, according to this stance, irrelevant – for the loss of freedom for the living is intrinsically much worse. We may wonder how that is known.

People, it is also argued, should be at liberty to take risks. Even in a pandemic, liberty requires that people be free to attend mass gatherings, be they at concerts, football matches or religious festivities: attendees wittingly accept that they are at risk from each other and take that risk. That thinking, however, ignores consequential risks to society, to millions of others who are risk averse – unless, astonishingly, mass-gathering attendees will inter-act with no other people when elsewhere, and if taken ill with Covid, will have no need of medical services.

Let us reflect more closely on the 'glory of freedom' – with people being free to do as they want and, I should add, free not to do what they want to do. That cannot be seriously held without caveats: even the most extreme libertarians support laws against intentionally killing non-consenting people; they sup-port laws to ensure that people drive on the same side of the road. Libertarians are not usually committed to anarchism's 'no government'.

Here is Hobbes again – describing life without government, in the 'State of Nature':

> In such condition there is no place for industry, because the fruit thereof is uncertain: and consequently no culture of the earth; no navigation, nor use of the commodities that may be imported by sea, no commodious building; no instruments of moving and removing such things as require much force; no knowledge of the face of the earth; no account of time; no arts; no letters; no society; and which is worst of all, continual fear,

and danger of violent death; and the life of man, solitary, poor, nasty, brutish, and short.

I cannot resist adding the reply, 'Thomas, it could be worse; the life of man could be solitary, poor, nasty, brutish – and long.'

THE GLORY OF LIBERTY, OF FREEDOM

People speak glowingly of liberty, freedom, yet what is meant? Why is it so prized? The terms are normally synonymous, though 'liberty' may direct us to where the law is silent.

Negative liberty is reduced by external constraints on my doing what I may choose to do. My liberty is restricted, for example, if laws exist against my saying whatever I think, whether or not I want to say what I think. I am still to some degree free to say what I think, but if I do, I suffer the burden of punishment. The freedom to shop does not count for much, if I lack money to buy. The valuable condition here would need to be not just negative liberty but **effective liberty** – something often forgotten by certain lovers of freedom.

Positive liberty is reduced – to a greater or lesser degree – by the extent to which I lack mastery of myself. I may fail to control my gambling addiction; to that extent, I am not free. Restrictions on negative liberty regarding gambling opportunities may aid my self-mastery. If I identify with gambling desires and object to the restrictions on my negative liberty, am I yet master of myself?

Autonomy (Greek: *autos*, self; *nomos*, law) overlaps with positive liberty. It is often associated with Kant's idea that I, as rational subject, set the laws and thus rule over myself, as subjected to those laws.

'Forced to be free' derives from Jean-Jacques Rousseau. I am acting freely when acting in my best interests, and those interests, it is curiously claimed, coincide with society's. If I am blind to that, then society's impositions on me may be required to set me free. Even though I think I am coerced, in fact I am free.

Life goes better for most human beings when in a law-governed society. The puzzle is which laws are justified and, ignoring the democratic dimension of lawmaking, that leads to questions about harms. Which harms are, so to speak, sufficiently harmful that protective legislation is needed? Further, should harms ultimately be cashed solely in terms of loss of freedom?

That latter question surely requires 'no'. What is bad about some illnesses is not (just) the loss (if any) of freedom, but the pain involved, the indignity and so forth. Even if freedom loss is always harmful – please see the boxed mention of gambling – we have complications of degrees of harm and relevancies of responsibility. For example, some liberty lovers railed against lockdowns because people were 'held captive' at home, yet many of those lovers railed not at all at the plight of millions held captive pre-Covid because of poverty. Does poverty not count as a harm, or does it count only if undeserved? And how would what is deserved be identified? Some rail against redistributive taxation as violating their freedom to do as they please with their money; they ignore how others' freedoms are curtailed if government-funded medical care and welfare benefits are lacking.

Many, outraged at the loss of freedom through lockdowns, have opposed lockdowns because the disadvantaged and other groups have been disproportionately harmed. That is true – they have – yet some who argued thus had previously supported government policies that disproportionately harmed those groups. The some, over the years in Britain, have supported, for example, radical cuts in local authority funding, leading to inadequacies in social care, greater homelessness and the closure of libraries and community centres – all having most impact on deprived areas and disadvantaged groups. It was curious that – taking another example – prior to the pandemic, a greater increase in NHS funding was apparently impossible, as if needing a magic money tree to be shaken, yet during the height of the pandemic in Britain, the money tree suddenly flourished and its shaking generated increased funding. Humanists would at least demand consistency in attempted justifications of such discrepancies.

Pan-deception and 'catastrophic moral failure'

A distinctive mantra is: 'No one is safe until everyone is safe.' It arrives courtesy of Pascal Soriot, chief executive officer, AstraZeneca, and it is endorsed by health experts, EU leaders, UK ministers, the US president (well, post-Trump) and others.

It is false. Some people possess natural immunity. It is misleading because the viral risks to millions are negligible compared to the risks to other millions. It is also misleading because millions of people are effectively vaccinated whereas millions are vaccinated not at all.

True, we may respect the mantra if implicitly qualified by 'for the most part'. Context sometimes justifies exaggeration: there can be exaggeration for ease (no space for caveats on banners) or to motivate people in the right direction – though, sometimes, in the wrong. Let us not fall for the idea that our liberal democracies – and humanists – always respect honesty. Consider our numerous consents, when engaging in internet searches, taking on mobile phone contracts or signing up for credit cards. How many people who tick boxes confirming that they have read and understood all the terms and conditions have in fact read all the terms and conditions, let alone understood them all? We wittingly accept, dare I say, an institutionalized lying.

Caveats aside, 'No one is safe until everyone is safe' possesses two types of justification. They are not incompatible. On the one hand, it could manifest enlightened self-interest. We are only eager that others be safely virus-free for otherwise they expose us to infection or burden our public services. On the other hand, many humanists hold the ethical stance to be distinct from self-interest: we should be concerned for the safety of others for their sake. That rests on fellow feeling, a sense of a common humanity and, yes, possesses the luxury extra of probably benefiting us. The stance promotes equitable treatment to the benefit of all.

Whether the focus be self-interest or other-interest, the concern was that nations – as with individuals – cannot or ought not to go it alone in virus battles. Again, we meet deceit: wealthy countries paid only lip service to the imperative that worldwide the most vulnerable and workers most likely to be exposed should have vaccination priority over others. True, within wealthy countries vaccination priority was typically given to the vulnerable, but regarding the worldwide position – and contrary to what was claimed as so vital – vaccination programmes in wealthy countries then moved to covering the less vulnerable and young, leaving even those most at risk in low-income countries largely unvaccinated. By late 2021, well over 80% of the UK's adult population had received two doses of the vaccine, whereas African countries were typically at figures easily below 5%.

That unfairness in vaccination distribution was deemed a 'catastrophic moral failure' by Tedros Adhanom Ghebreyesus, head of the World Health Organization.

Once again, slogans are shown often to be misleading or unhelpful. We earlier saw muddles over quite what the freedom mantra amounts to; here we have muddles concerning preferences, discriminations and equal treatment. Normally, we give priority to our children, our parents, our friends, over other individuals, unless offering services to the public at large. Further, we discriminate in favour of ourselves; we prefer luxuries for ourselves over using resources to pay for life-preserving essentials for disadvantaged others. Ought we to do so?

Humanist values cannot be held in a completely detached manner. We may well wonder what life would be like if we adopted a totally detached attitude to people in all our relationships or, for that matter, to projects – from saving the whale to supporting the arts to funding clean water initiatives – in determining what ought to be done.

Similarly, preferences – partialities, prejudices – operate at the international level. Nation states have preferences over who may be permitted residency, which asylum seekers are to be accepted – and who should be vaccinated first. It is all very well to speak of being 'fair', but what constitutes fairness in these contexts? Humanists – as all of us – should at least recognize that mantras in favour of respect, fairness and liberty are not themselves sufficient to show what should be done and how far our attachments should take priority over detached perspectives – and how far morally they ought not. Similar fairness puzzles arise for governments and pharmaceutical companies over companies' duties regarding vaccination production – pricing, research programmes, distribution policies – as indeed regarding access to many life-enhancing treatments.

The obscurity of the fairness plea is also shown by the complaint that Covid-19 restrictions unfairly harmed the young far more than the elderly. There are, though, different prospects for different groups at different ages with different lifespans and in different circumstances. Lives should probably be assessed over the whole: if so assessed, any fairness calculation would need account of how things were for the elderly when young – when lacking many benefits accepted as normal or necessary by the young of today. 'Intergenerational justice' is a fine phrase, but its application is far from clear.

Focus on the young, reasonably enough, brings us to climate change worries, for we are in the main looking some decades ahead and further. Allow me the speculation that people currently in their seventies and beyond will themselves be largely unaffected.

Climate change and future lives

There is considerable evidence accepted by the majority of scientists that global warming means that 'unless something is done' life is going to be much worse for most human beings – and, we may add, for many other species, though some may flourish; indeed, new species may evolve as a result. With sea levels rising, some lands will no longer be habitable; there will be desperate migrations to areas less affected, thus disturbing populations already under some stress from climate extremes.

The term 'Anthropocene Epoch' has been somewhat casually coined to identify the period when human activities – deforestation, mining and unsustainable agriculture – have started significantly to affect the earth's climate and ecosystems. Some doubts exist, though, regarding the quantitative magnitude of anthropogenic warming relative to natural non-human factors; and, of course, a scientific consensus may receive subsequent revision – even radical revision. Who knows how things may change?

The central worry is curious for it is directed towards the welfare of future generations – of billions of people who do not yet exist – though, true, some lives already suffer because of floods, droughts, wildfires and the like brought on by the extended climate extremes. Furthermore, the measures to reduce global warming will affect most people, one way or another.

Some in wealthy countries will benefit. Policies to reduce carbon dioxide and methane emissions, despite being likely to restrict car use, meat consumption and international flights – and hence trade and cheap imports – may lead to healthier lives, with less pollution and fewer toxins in foods, and may prevent further decline in biodiversity, perhaps even increasing the diversity.

Only a status quo bias could generate objections to that, assuming measures are in place to help the poorest. Yes, that is a big and probably wildly optimistic humanist assumption.

Many in the lowest-income countries will suffer. First, foreign aid may be for emission reduction, endangering means of livelihoods. Secondly, selling goods abroad may become more difficult, if international trade is reduced. Thirdly, their economic development – infrastructure, housing, health services – may be slowed. Lest we forget, today's comfortable living in wealthy countries resulted from industrial developments started centuries ago; they have been the main contributors to the climate crisis in as far as human activity is indeed the cause. Wealthy countries are urging policies that will prevent the poorest from doing what in part led to the wealthy countries' wealth. Thus, we have another arena where one feels the need for fairness, yet with no clarity regarding what would constitute that fairness.

As with pandemic awareness, we may deploy a qualified mantra that no one is safe until everyone is safe. As with pandemic awareness, whatever is said, countries may seek to prioritize their own interests. Certain countries may argue that their emission reductions would make very little difference, ignoring how their reductions may set a good example to follow. Others may boast of their reductions, silent about the carbon content of their imports.

We see again how difficult it is properly to apply humanist values of fairness and welfare, even when considering existing people. We need, though, to throw future people into the calculation, if calculation is the way to go. How are future people affected by what is done now to reduce global warming?

Suppose nothing is done: millions of people will come into existence, many of whom will have climate crises with which to contend. Were those future people to look back, they may denigrate us for failing to prevent global warming. Had, though, preventive policies been followed, human activities would have been different and those particular future complainants would not have existed; yet most of them would probably be pleased to be alive rather than never to have been born. They may even have embraced new ways of living, looking back on our ways as quaint and our worries about future living as manifesting another status quo bias.

Let us underline the above thus. Excess consumption, resource depletion, pollution, landfills and so forth will harm future human beings – and indeed many other creatures. To reduce those harms, we should restrict family size: we should urge birth control or sterilization, discourage fertility treatments, encouraging adoption instead. That, of course, interferes with those religions that take to heart the biblical injunction 'go forth and multiply'; it also upsets humanists who, as well as perhaps fearing horrors of eugenics (please see Chapter 9), live by the unqualified 'glory of freedom' mantra. It also has the following outcome.

With procreation restrictions implemented, many people who would have existed will not exist – but those non-existents are in no position to argue that they have been harmed. How can non-existent individuals be harmed? Of course, the chances that any of us would come to be were astonishingly teeny. Which people happen to exist rests on contingencies such as a late train, the job offer, the evening's television schedule, excess alcohol – or length of lockdown – as well as many other unlikelihoods. There are, indeed, many, many chance contingencies in play.

Humanist values are much concerned with not harming people. Humanists, as also religious believers, are often morally moved by the Golden Rule (noted in Chapter 3): 'Do unto others as you would have them do unto you.' Future generations (ones that do not overlap with our existence) can do nothing for us now or ever. The Golden Rule, if grounded in reciprocation, clearly here lacks application. As the essayist Joseph Addison observed, 'We are always doing something for posterity, but I would fain see posterity doing something for us.'

That the Golden Rule cannot justify our concern for future generations does not establish no concern is justly needed. Humanists, on grounds of fairness, could see moral merit in the rule: do what you can for your successors as you would have had your predecessors do for you. However the concern is justified, some argue that ecocide – the mass damage and destruction of the natural living world – should be legally recognized as one of the 'crimes against humanity'.

Perhaps we do have duties towards whoever they are who will exist in the future – but in what way and how far into the future? 'Whoever they are in the future' may be too wide a designation regarding types of future individuals deserving of humanists' worries, not least because some scientists speculate on future 'life' extending far beyond human biology or evolution on Earth. They propose the likelihood of individuals or clouds of artificial intelligent life beyond human grasp – maybe already existing elsewhere in this universe so vast. Whether those existences should be deemed 'life', with consciousness, beliefs and intentions, is open to doubt. Concepts can be stretched so far that their sense and usefulness break down. If there should be human concern for that 'life' already existing, it should be concern over what concern – if that even makes sense – it may have for humanity. Let us, though, steer clear of those wild conjectures; there is enough trouble ahead in sorting out how humanist values may apply to predicted enhancements of human beings here on Earth – as we are to see.

9
Whither humanism?
Whither humanity?

I didn't come this far to come only this far.

Anon

Humanism is old hat – some increasingly argue. They provide a plethora of understandings, sometimes with hyphenated nuances, projecting forth a world of the posthuman, the post-human, of posthumanism and post-humanism; they treat of the transhuman, the trans-human, of transhumanism and trans-humanism. In addition, we encounter antihumanism, anti-humanism, immortalism and the philosophy of singularity. More terms could be added with a variety of nuanced meanings.

In the 1880s, Friedrich Nietzsche's Zarathustra was speaking of man as something that shall be overcome, as a rope tied between beast and 'overman' – a rope over an abyss. 'What is great in man is that he is a bridge and not an end.' Nietzsche's project is tied to a transvaluation of all values, thus it dismisses both humanist values and humanity's nature. It is, though, distant from many of today's transforming urges for biological changes whereby human happiness and liberal freedoms – typical humanist values – are invigorated.

Ideas, predictions, hopes and fears of human individuals going well beyond current capacities involve enhancements of biology – bionic limbs, genetic manipulations, bloodstreams carrying nanotechnological cell repairers, neurological circuits with microchip inserts – leading to expanded sense perceptions,

THE TERMINOLOGY TEASE

There is a motley collection of revised understandings of 'human' and 'humanism' with the prefix 'trans' or 'post'. Usages overlap. The following provides but a feel for the terminology. Allow me to urge the mantra (derived from Wittgenstein): don't ask for the meaning; look at the use.

Transhumanism, deployed first by Julian Huxley in 1957, focuses on how the human species should realize new possibilities and transcend itself. Dante Alighieri's *Divine Comedy* (c.1308–1321) introduced the Italian *trasumanar* to label the ascent from the terrestrial paradise to the celestial realm of the blessed.

Today's transhumanists often seek to liberate human beings from biological limits by means of science and technology, accelerating the evolution of intelligent life. The aim is usually to increase human happiness. Little steps may be by way of more efficient drugs to boost academic performance and microchip neurological inserts to carry 'memory' currently stored on mobile phones.

The singularity is sometimes taken to be the point when machines become more intelligent than humans, generating a runaway superintelligence, though sometimes for the point when humans secure immortality through technological advance, thus no longer being human as we know it. Hence, we meet posthumanism in one version.

Posthumanism, first actively discussed in the 1990s, may draw attention to the development of artificial intelligence whereby automata supersede the human species or intermesh with human biology, creating a new species. It is, though, often used to present a challenge to **exceptionalism**, the belief that there are sharp boundaries that must be preserved between human beings and other species.

greater intelligence, bigger leaps, faster runs and added longevities, even immortality. Some enthusiasts have ideals of dispensing with human biology altogether: our consciousness, memories and aims – our minds – are uploaded to digital clouds with who knows what outcome for personal identities. Transhumanism in its variety of forms offers the startling thought 'Whither humanity?'

Contrasting with those enhancements of human beings, enhanced to such an extent that they may be 'beyond human' and hence, in a sense, post-human, the focus may be on altering perspectives on human beings. The altered perspectives arise through greater evidence and more sensitive reflection on non-human species and the globe's biodiversity – even the possibility of new forms of life such as intelligent automata. Humanist ideas and ideals of the human species as exceptional are rejected. Thus, posthumanism can lead to the question 'Whither humanism?'

Let us engage the transformational – initially via an unusual and frightening example – before confronting posthumanist doubts on human exceptionalism.

Respecting Rebekah?

Rebekah holds humanist values, whether or not she knows them as such. She is keen on people being free to act as they please – always, of course, so long as not harming others – and she is kind and helpful. She possesses a strong sense of the personal and private, of how our lives ought not to be spied upon by others or, for that matter, by divine omnipresence. She has nothing to hide; she does not lurk behind fictious names, stolen identities or off-shore corporations. She simply dislikes her movements tracked, her medical records treated as commercial products, her phone calls monitored.

When out and about, she is aware of CCTV watching her; she is also aware of how she is often unaware of such tracking. When she uses her phone or laptop, her texts, conversations and locations can all be traced. She steers clear of Twitter, Instagram and similar, yet corporations and governments still manage to collect data on her purchases, interests and internet searches. She is bombarded with advertisements tempting her to buy; she receives texts from the political and the seemingly non-political urging her support. Even at home, curtains closed, she senses surveillance. Delivery drones pass by her window; who knows quite what they record?

In summary, she lives in a world dominated by an advanced capitalism that profits through surveillance of, and big data on, billions of people as consumers. Unless she excludes herself from the digital society – millions are excluded because lacking competence or financial resources – she is exposed to numerous intrusions and, indeed, the dangers of being hacked. For her to conduct her life as she wants, she needs to enter the public world to meet friends, enjoy walks, hear the news and so forth. She is no lover of eternal lockdowns, of pixel-filled screens courtesy of Zoom, Microsoft Teams or some other technological 'contact'. She loves life; she loves love; she is sociable.

One hundred years ago, or even more recently, Rebekah would have found herself oppressed differently, by way of severe restrictions on employments, financial independence, expressions of sexuality and avoidance of unwanted pregnancies. She would have lacked today's easy communications, benefits of medical advance, essential services on tap – and favourite music at the flip of a switch.

★ ★ ★

Let us project Rebekah's life forward, using a global corporation, AlwaysGloballyHere4U (AGH), a company ever eager to enhance life through cyber developments.

AGH knows Rebekah's location. When she checks her phone, there appear tempting offers available from shops nearby. That advertising is, though, so old-fashioned; she has to hear the alert, look at the screen and in so doing, photons strike her optic nerve, causing neurological changes – cellular reactions, electrical pulses – that have wonderful names and complicated measures known only to neurologists. The outcome is that she thinks, 'Ah, let's take a look, I fancy some new shoes' and enters the shop; or maybe she thinks, 'Yet more consumerism' and walks on by – refusing to buy.

AGH takes matters further. The new AGH Helper 'phone' cuts out the middle-man, so to speak; it directly causes the neurological changes that provide awareness of the enticing messages. In early versions, Rebekah recognizes the messages as alien, as derived from the device. That recognition is, of course, also grounded in neurological changes. Upgraded Helpers have the messages transmitted with external markers nullified; the messages cross Rebekah's mind just as thoughts often arise unbidden. So far, Rebekah possesses the possibility of 'resisting' the temptations; a further Helper upgrade erases resistances.

Carrying a device around carries risks for AGH. Rebekah may lose it, drop it or smash it in rebellious rage. Happily for AGH, its network's recognitional capacities become so advanced – by satellite, drones or means yet developed – that Rebekah is spotted wherever she is, her 'private' thoughts scanned, uploaded to the network and her neurological circuits then modified directly as AGH determines. Rebekah's individuality (whatever remains of that) is more and more reduced; in fact, anyone with her interests, resources and locations will unwittingly act in the same way, as AGH requires.

Rebekah set off as a decent individual with humanist values and concerns, but they too are vulnerable to AGH's cellular transmissions. Maybe she finds herself committed to a morality based on self-interest and disparagement of the disadvantaged; perhaps, paradoxically, she is now a keen libertarian, glorifying untrammelled 'free markets' as promoted by AGH. Perhaps she now settles for virtual reality, lacking desire to go out and about and meet friends face to biological face, without artificial aids, save maybe glasses and similar.

Rebekah has unwittingly lost her autonomy. She is but an automaton, buffeted by the inputs courtesy of AGH. She has, in a serious way, lost her mind, her self, her privacy, though her biological appearance remains much the same. Regarding what is of considerable importance to being human, she is transhuman or, more accurately, she is post-human, no human at all in what matters.

This is no wild speculation. Eric Schmidt, then chairman of Google, spoke of how 'you won't even sense it', when attending to interactions of sensors and devices as we move through the world. 'Big tech' leaders speak of how the technologies will weave themselves into everyday life until they and it are indistinguishable. Perhaps it is unlikely that AGH would be the sole global business of this ilk. That offers no comfort. Rebekah's psychological life would be battered by competing inputs of beliefs and desires that she wrongly felt to be hers.

Let us not be shocked by the scenario. We all frequently coax and cajole others into our ways of thinking, as others do us in return. Modifications of people's desires and beliefs by businesses have been crudely achieved through bill posters, 'must have' latest designs and amazing offers. Even the aroma of percolating coffee is known to make the apartment for sale more appealing. AGH has just taken steps further – well, yes, exceedingly further.

Transhumans without the humanity

With liberty to the fore, humanists – and many non-humanists – casually promote the idea of corporate freedoms, yet in the Rebekah tale those freedoms have gone too far, far too far. The tale could be run such that people's behaviour is best understood as of just one mind, the AGH mind, with Rebekah's 'own' thoughts (as she thinks of them) combined with others' 'own' thoughts. It could be run such that certain groups accept, even welcome, a position as slaves. The intrusions – say, by a benign government – could secure desirable outputs with people finding themselves praising humanist values, respecting others and improving the lot of the most disadvantaged.

Run the tale anyway you want, it casts doubt on our grasp of autonomy, freedom and 'our' authentic reasons, beliefs and desires. Our psychological states (and, for that matter, those of AGH's directors and scientists who developed the Helper) result from sequences of neurological changes; it is difficult to see how 'we' control them. A complex medley of factors affects what we believe, desire and do; all that may generate uncertainty about outcome, but it does not show that what happens is uncertain or rests on 'our' free choices. Objectors to the implied determinism may draw attention to subatomic randomness underlying the neurology; but whatever can be made of that? Our autonomy or freedom of choice is not to be grasped as mere randomness.

We live lives, it seems, grounded in illusion. Our understanding of self and autonomy is chaotic: a sceptical conclusion repugnant to humanists and others. That reasoning also, of course, is vulnerable to sceptical attack – as is the conclusion about its vulnerability. Reasoning needs to be assessed for soundness – is it any good? – yet reasonings, given current understandings, ones typically adopted by humanists, are grounded in neurological changes. Those changes – chemical releases, electrical transmissions – know no soundness or unsoundness, no right or wrong. Indeed, the supposition that some neurons firing away 'know' anything at all is as nonsensical as supposing this pebble on the seashore is in the know about ocean waves.

This is not good news for humanists; it is not good news for anyone. What is good news is that we cannot live the life of a sceptic, be the scepticism about the self, free will or good reasoning. Mundanely, even if everything is determined and seen by the likes of AGH – or, for that matter, by divine decision or by our nature and nurture – we have yet to 'decide' whether to wear the red outfit or the blue for the dinner this evening. Is there, though, any good reason, apart from AGH's intent, why we treat the AGH impositions as undermining our autonomy, yet not those of everyday nature and nurture?

Enhancements: flying too close to the sun?

Let us put aside the sceptical puzzle concerning our autonomy; let us return to human life as we take it to be. Transformations for improvement are built into humanism. Pico della Mirandola – encountered in Chapter 1 – has the creator telling Adam, 'Thou, constrained by no limits … shalt ordain for thyself the limits of thy nature,' whereas all other beings are constrained within the bounds of laws.

Humanist-inspired improvements of people's lives have typically been through education, greater welfare and changes in social expectations. Proposed or foreseen technological changes are developments in 'the same spirit', freely chosen, presenting us with 'transhumans'. Contact lenses considerably benefit eyesight; what's wrong with enhancements by means of zoom and camera facilities built within eyes? Handheld calculators have aided many people arithmetically stressed and distressed; microchips neurologically inserted could enable immediate relaxed completion of calculations 'from within'. Let us cast asunder bulky headphones and small earphones that are wont to slip out; we choose neurological implants for streaming music. Coffee has kept many of us going; slow-releasing stimulants built into our biology may transform us further for the better – so the story goes.

Despite obvious cases of improvement, many resist going 'too far', but what counts as 'too far'? After all, one should also resist not going far enough. One suggested control is not going beyond what is natural, normal or healthy. Some draw a distinction between 'treatments' (good) and 'enhancements' (bad).

Religious believers may rely on divine guidance here: interfering with human biology to overcome diseases, accidents and failings is praised, but going beyond is wrong. Lacking divine guidance, it is difficult for humanists to judge what constitutes a natural, normal, healthy human, and why, whatever that constitution is, it merits no improvement.

Religions promote the thought that human nature is a divine gift; meddling dishonours God. Humanism has no truck with that. On a mundane level, people eagerly meddle by way of buying books on 'self-improvement'. Naturally, humanists will show caution in any tamperings with nature, fearing unintended bad consequences. Certain humanists may even see the natural as having its own value and resist interfering on that basis, but that is no stable position. Let us remember, human beings and their interventions are part of what is natural. Humans evolved – just as did other species – through natural selection. Humanists have no room for divine sparks; they are not given to believing that evolution has generated human beings as supernatural beings or beings beyond nature, as if of a *supra*natural species.

The human condition is far from ideal: there are many undesirable features and limits. Humanists, it would seem, cannot have any well-grounded intrinsic objections to people enhancing physical capabilities and forms; such enhancements offer 'morphological freedom'. Similarly, dangers of unforeseen consequences aside, the humanist liberal stance should not conflict with people being at liberty to develop improved cognitive capabilities and desirable emotions. Of course, some of us may be wary; some of us may, remembering the Preface, settle for and even embrace Kant's crooked timber.

★   ★   ★

Assuming some clarity over what counts as improvements, two key questions arise. Who is doing the improvements for whom? What are the effects on others and on society? Consider designer babies: the idea can give rise to shrieks of 'eugenics'. The term means 'good births', but there is the associated horror of the attempted genocide of all of Jewish descent and an increasing awareness of how the United Kingdom, the United States and others historically have far from clean hands with regard to compulsory sterilization programmes and genocidal aims.

What, though, are the objections to a 'liberal eugenics' where people possess the freedom to choose how to enhance lives of future children? Usually, we praise parents who do the best for their children by way of education, health and home. 'Designer babies' sums up parents improving the lot of their children by prior genetic changes. The embryos have no say in the design, but today's children have no say regarding their genetic nature and how they are initially nurtured.

There are risks. Some parents may be obsessed with their offspring becoming outstanding tennis players or highly motivated to become rich – or amazingly intelligent, beautiful or modest. Had genetic enhancers existed in Victorian days, parents may have lined up foetuses for the set of genes that, in combination with appropriate nurturing, would lead to them being good God-fearing Christians. Authorities may have ensured that the poor gave birth to offspring with talents for chimney sweeping or factory work without complaint. Whatever the manipulations, a likely objection, as already implied, is that the children's future free choices will have been eroded; we are returned, though, to the illusion exposed by the Rebekah tale. It is as if people believe children's 'natural' genetic natures to be under the children's control.

Many people – humanists and all – proclaim commitment to 'equal opportunities' while fighting to secure competitive advantage for their own children. Genetic engineering, unless state run with proper universal provision, would, no doubt, be available only to the wealthy, well-connected or articulate; thus, there could develop a distinctive super-bred ruling class. The human species could develop into two distinct populations. That would not be a humanist project.

Genuine humanist motives exist, of course, for promoting fairness and equal opportunities. Genetic engineering could be aimed for the benefit of all; but how would that work? Individuals do not set off equally in life; to overcome that, we should need equality in education, housing, parental concern and so forth. Were that achieved – and what sort of world would that be? – children would still differ in genetic make-up, in potentiality and motivation for success in athletics, algebra and arduous labour. The equality aim would then need to be to make 'all foetuses equal'. If successful, consider the outcome. Would the sole differences between people – putting matters of sexual differences to one side – then rest on external fortunes or misfortunes; some happen to be caught in a tsunami, some not?

Puzzlingly, humanists live with a mish-mash of inequalities, partialities and desires that they know ought to be overcome – but not overcome too much.

Exceptionalism

The preceding has raised dangers and incoherences in quests for enhanced human living. The enhancements, good or bad, may be so radical that they present as 'post-human'. Posthumanism, though, is often understood as rejecting any humanist or trans-humanist commitment to human beings as exceptional and superior to all other (known) species. The topic is of particular importance both to humanism as a doctrine and to humanists – indeed to all of us – regarding how non-human creatures ought to be treated. Let us focus on human beings as they are before we gesture towards how the arguments hold up were humans to be 'superly' transformed.

The belief that human beings are creatures uniquely endowed with superior capacities for reason, self-reflection and morality has been grounded in commitment to their having been created by God in God's image. Humanists lack recourse to that divine grounding; they rely on the evidence.

Obviously, there are many similarities and dissimilarities, to varying degrees, between human beings and other creatures. We gradually learn more and more about them. We are impressed not solely by the ways of dolphins, gorillas and chimps, but also by the talents of octopuses, corvids and ant communities. There are manifest differences concerning reason, self-reflection and creativity; human beings typically distinguish between what they want to do and what they ought to do. We anguish about how to treat other animals; other animals do not (usually, if ever) anguish about how to treat us, as individuals or as a species – or, indeed, how to treat other species and their members.

The term 'humanism' may suggest that humanist values must be solely human centred. Even if that is true – and it is not – it does not follow that humanists see no value in non-human creatures. It does not follow for the simple reason that considerable elements of the non-human world are essential for human flourishing: non-humans (and much else) possess at least instrumental value for humans. Thus we meet Kant again:

> When [man] first said to the sheep, 'the pelt which you wear was given to you by nature not for your own use, but for mine' and took it from the sheep to wear it himself, he became aware of a prerogative which, by his nature, he enjoyed over all the animals.

For Kant, we owe duties only indirectly to animals; we demean ourselves by causing them unnecessary pain. If mistreating them, we may progress to mistreating human beings. Human exceptionalism comes to the fore on Kant's view – and that of many humanists – because human beings, unlike non-humans, are not to be treated solely as means to an end (a stance outlined in Chapter 4). On this view, humans are exceptional.

Contrasting with Kant's approach, humanists of a basic utilitarian glow have direct regard for animals as for human beings. When judging either, the morally relevant mantra is Jeremy Bentham's 'Can they suffer?' The utilitarian calculation for maximizing happiness (also discussed in Chapter 4) includes the sufferings and pleasures of all creatures.

Humanists value compassion. Many people readily and rightly feel compassion towards non-human animals – well, certain ones – concerned for their sake, not just for their usefulness for human welfare. It need not be *despite* being humanist that humanists have regard for non-human animals; it can be *because* they are humanists. Here, though, is Archy bemoaning his lot, as a Latin poet reincarnated as cockroach:

> as a representative
> of the insect world
> i have often wondered
> on what man bases his claims
> to superiority
> everything he knows he has had
> to learn whereas we insects are born
> knowing everything we need to know

Archy rails against humans with their preferences for beautiful butterflies over cockroaches; he complains that by swatting flies they do spiders and their children out of supper – and so forth.

However things are with cockroaches, spiders and flies, many non-human animals have subjective experiences, goals and interests even though they cannot verbally express them; they are sentient. I have interests – in certain of my desires being satisfied, in my life continuing – and I justifiably expect other human beings to have regard for my interests just as I should have for theirs. To be consistent, I ought also to have regard for other creatures and their interests. I ought not to dismiss those other creatures merely because they cannot (usually) reciprocate.

The human preference is typically for saving human lives over lives of others. That may not be sheer prejudice 'for our own'. Perhaps human lives matter more because of the greater potential richness, but by what objective measure? Within the human species, from the human perspective, some members' lives may be enriched were they to read philosophy, listen to Schubert's lieder or help the dispossessed. It would, though, be nonsense to argue that the lives of elephants, eagles and eels – even gorillas – would be enriched by philosophy, Schubert's lieder or helping the dispossessed. That would be no life at all for them. True, a few general and basic enrichments can work across species: for example, easy access to food.

This may suggest that we should be as much concerned about saving lives of corvids, cattle and cuttlefish as of human beings – unless we justify our preferential attachment to the human species, a speciesism, as akin to that for our family over others (please see Chapter 6): a family-ism. If that justification fails, then we are pushed back, by consistency, into having as much concern for saving the lives of other sentient creatures, of those that have interests and interest in their lives continuing, as saving human lives – or are we?

On the one hand, that demand for consistency could just be something that matters to us, from our human perspective; perhaps our lives could be enriched further by not caring for consistency when dealing with other species. We should care for consistency only when it aids our flourishing – for example, in engineering, accountancy and law, even philosophy. On the other hand, perhaps consistency is an objective value and not valuable solely from our perspective: consistency is good – and often morally good, full stop. With that foothold, maybe we can spot other objective values, one of them being the greater value of creatures who can spot and have regard for such values – thus the greater value in typically saving human lives over, say, the lives of hyenas.

Some may argue that such considerations are irrelevant because one day there will be a post-human species possessed of accelerating superintelligence, be it through technological advances or AGH-style intrusions. We should, though, handle such thinking with care. Can we even conceptualize how 'super-intelligence' could determine the true nature of humanist values and how those values should be measured against each other? What sense is there in superintelligence grasping not merely what it is like to be a bat, baboon or blackbird, but how their lives should be valued? Of course, answers may be in terms of why expect that we, mere human beings as currently constituted, can grasp the unfathomable. Such answers may remind us of religious appeals to 'trust in God'; his ways are bound to be mysterious to mere humans. That reminder of those appeals should lack appeal to humanists; humanists should resist faith in unknown and unknowable future post-human superintelligent species.

Extinction

Even if now or in the future, human beings are, in an objective sense, more valuable than other creatures, it does not follow that they ought not to promote the well-being of those individual non-human others for their sake. That differs from concern for the species. A few people devote their lives to saving the whale. Sometimes they have a particular whale in mind to save, but the devotion is for the well-being of the species. It is difficult, though, to make sense of a species, qua species, as having interests from its perspective. A species has no perspective.

Leslie Stephen, father of Virginia Woolf, quipped 'The pig has a stronger interest than anyone in the demand for bacon. If all the world were Jewish, there would be no pigs at all.' Use of '*the* pig' may hide the fact that what is good for the individual can differ from what is good for the breed or species. For a species to flourish, there may need to be a culling; that is hardly in the interests of those members killed.

The ever-increasing concern for biodiversity – for preservation of species; regret at the loss of so many – may once again be motivated by concern for the interests of human beings. The radical decline in insects through agricultural intensification reduces food supply for birds, reptiles and fish, thus eventually endangering human beings. The mosquito genome project aims at eliminating malarial mosquitoes. That would be of considerable benefit to millions of people; but who knows how the elimination may affect the great chain of being, delivering harms to human beings in the long run?

Even if the diversity of species, as it currently exists, is not necessary for human existence – we exist despite the dodo's extinction – human beings enjoy knowing that a diversity of species exists. Preservation of species may also aid medicinal discoveries. However much some people may have wanted the extinction of poisonous snakes, their venom's anticoagulant properties have proved valuable in developments of certain life-saving drugs.

★　★　★

Human beings are exceptional; they can see themselves as stewards of nature, having at least some respect these days for non-human creatures and some recognition of the intrinsic value of diverse species existing. We face here more bafflement: helping the well-being of these hungry lions means closing our eyes to the well-being of those gazelles about to be gnawed to painful deaths. Humanists – unlike, according to many believers, God, the divine designer – would not have started from here, with a living world dependent on immense suffering. Should humanists therefore seek the gradual extinction of carnivores and of meat-eating by humans – and urge the good living of herbivores?

What, though, would justify human beings taking on that role and with what unforeseen consequences for biodiversity?

Let us own up. We human beings are responsible for many disasters that befall – wait for it – human beings. Here is Thomas Malthus, writing in the late eighteenth century, well before global warming awareness:

> The power of population is so superior to the power in the earth to produce subsistence for man, that premature death must in some shape or other visit the human race. The vices of mankind are active and able ministers of depopulation. They are the precursors in the great army of destruction; and often finish the dreadful work themselves.

Should those vices fail to depopulate, then 'sickly seasons, epidemics, pestilence, and plague [will] advance in terrific array, and sweep off their thousands and tens of thousands.' In case appropriate depopulation is yet incomplete, 'gigantic inevitable famine stalks in the rear, and with one mighty blow, levels the population with the food of the world.'

There is no need to examine here Malthus's agricultural assumptions or the current consensus on how best to handle global warming. What we do know is that, given finite resources, there is an upper limit on the number of people who could exist at any given time and a much, much, much lower limit if the lives are to be worth living. The human population will be limited, be it through wars, pandemics, global warming, starvation – or birth controls, compelled or voluntary.

Let us own up further. We human beings are responsible for many disasters that befall other species. Noise of oil tankers disorientate whales; light pollution baffles birds; microplastics damage coral reefs, insects and fish. What is best overall for other species and the planet could well be the extinction of human beings. That could scarcely be a humanist project – or could it?

In view of vast sufferings of non-human creatures, may not earth be at its most desirable, at its most beautiful, with sunsets, storms and ocean roars, with lapping waves, forest glades and wildflower meadows, yet devoid of sentient beings, of all beings that could suffer? Were that possible, that could scarcely be a humanist project – or could it?

Arthur Schopenhauer, writing in the early nineteenth century, understood human lives as essentially racked with sufferings. Even ignoring illnesses, dying and associated miseries, even ignoring wars, deliberate torturings and natural disasters, everyday living consists of considerable suffering – and not just from toothache, indigestion and love affairs. We strive to achieve – that is suffering enough – and eventually undergo pains of failure or pains of success's bleak boredom before striving afresh. Many people hope that things will go better for their children; but that passes the buck. They too will undergo the sufferings and maybe attempted buck-passing.

The chorus in Sophocles' *Oedipus at Colonus* proclaims: the happiest (the blessed) are those 'not to have been born'. That provocative thought, noted earlier (in Chapter 7), merits the Jewish quip, 'Who is so lucky? Not one in a hundred thousand.'

★　★　★

David Hume, when suffering melancholic clouds of philosophic doubt, of the scepticism generated by his reasoning, turned away. I picture him leaving his study, closing the door. 'I dine, I play a game of backgammon, I converse, and am merry with my friends,' he wrote. There we see humanism's fellow feeling at play. Reasoning needs to know its place.

Having come this far, humanity yet has far to go. Of course, there will be an end. It is not, though, a matter of waiting to see, but of waiting – and not seeing.

Epilogue

Human that we are ... *Humans* that we are ...

Here is a tribute to humanity. When under dictatorial rule, with free speech much constrained, a young intellectual mimed; he mimed in a public square. He mimed a protest speech, a speech without words. People drew round to watch and listen; to watch the expressive gestures, the flicker of tongue, the mouthing lips; to listen to – silence. The authorities also watched and listened, but did nothing.

The incident – 1986, Zagreb, Yugoslavia – says much. It is a tribute to humanity: the young man's ingenuity, courage and force for freedom. It may also be condemnation of humanity: the authorities' desire for power, conformity, repression. The incident displays human absurdity – a protest speech without words. A protest was being made, as all could tell. Yet the law – *the law* – remained unbroken. The protestor obeyed the law's demand not to speak, yet spoke. The police were dutiful in stopping protest, yet permitted protest.

Our humanity enables us to see our lives as filled with incongruities and tensions such as the above – yet also with aspirations and achievements, also as above. Our humanity encourages a smile, perhaps even when facing extinction.

Were this a musical book, readers would now hear Thomas Tallis's *Spem in alium*, the choir's voices lifting us to heavens of hope, the breadth of beauty. Humanists have no problem with being moved by religious music.

Were this book a carpet of magic, we should fly over the destitute and impoverished. Humanists do not shield their eyes from life's woes, tragedies and sheer horrors often deliberately inflicted by human beings. Humanists can be angry at humanity's inhumanity.

Were this a musical, magical carpet, we should be enveloped by the absurdity – the obscenity – of our well-fed lives, in choral heavens, while others struggle for breath. *I can't go on. I'll go on.*

In bleak weakness, some despair to live well, with so much suffering elsewhere – indeed, with just one person suffering elsewhere. In glowing strength, many do what they can for others, while living the best they can for themselves. Humanists come in both varieties; both varieties manifest fellow feeling. Humanists come as optimists and as pessimists about what may be achieved. My path is more the pessimist, but whatever we humanists do, whatever tangles we live, whatever stances we adopt – whatever slight angles we stand to the universe – we know they are our own. There is no one out there, in a heaven or hell, to whom to pass the buck.

Socrates held that the unexamined life is not worth living. True or not, humanism encourages at least some examining. In so doing, humanism may heighten awareness of life's absurdities – for, like the protestor who spoke protest without speaking, we are most significant when lost in something, the large or the small. We may lose ourselves in humanitarian projects, yet also simply in friendship; in awesome opera, yet also tinkling tunes on the piano; in fiery crocosmia, yet also in tiny speedwell.

Serious points can be made with irony: witness the humour and humanity of Rupert Brooke overleaf.

The book's overarching epigram is: let us be human.

What else can we be?

Heaven

Fish (fly-replete, in depth of June,
Dawdling away their wat'ry noon)
Ponder deep wisdom, dark or clear,
Each secret fishy hope or fear.
Fish say, they have their Stream and Pond;
But is there anything Beyond?
This life cannot be All, they swear,
For how unpleasant, if it were!
One may not doubt that, somehow, Good
Shall come of Water and of Mud;
And, sure, the reverent eye must see
A Purpose in Liquidity.
We darkly know, by Faith we cry,
The future is not Wholly Dry.
Mud unto mud!—Death eddies near—
Not here the appointed End, not here!
But somewhere, beyond Space and Time,
Is wetter water, slimier slime!
And there (they trust) there swimmeth One
Who swam ere rivers were begun,
Immense, of fishy form and mind,
Squamous, omnipotent, and kind;
And under that Almighty Fin,
The littlest fish may enter in.
Oh! never fly conceals a hook,
Fish say, in the Eternal Brook,
But more than mundane weeds are there,
And mud, celestially fair;
Fat caterpillars drift around,
And Paradisal grubs are found;
Unfading moths, immortal flies,
And the worm that never dies.
And in that Heaven of all their wish,
There shall be no more land, say fish.

Rupert Brooke

Acknowledgements

As part of the Humanist Philosophers' Group, when writing the book's first edition, I received considerable stimulation from many humanist colleagues. I thank them all. I am also especially grateful to Michael Clark, Laurence Goldstein, Brendan Larvor and Richard Norman for commenting on some portions of early drafts. I thank too anonymous readers.

Ardon Lyon merits my special gratitude for his meticulous care, well beyond the call of friendship, let alone duty, in commenting, laughing, shrieking, muttering – well, doing something – at nearly every sentence of the whole manuscript, either in agreement, disagreement, outrage, incomprehension, surprise or amusement – and sometimes all these things at once. Regarding more practical, sustaining and continuing matters, I am especially indebted to Angela Joy Harvey.

For some scriptural details and encouragement, I am very grateful to Andrew Harvey; for some classical references, Sir David Blatherwick; for some humanist references, Andrew Copson; for awareness of humanistic psychology, Emilie Crossley; and for some practical support, Malcolm Fleming, Donika Jordan, Marsha Ozo and Bernie Haaser. Of course, this book would not exist but for Martha Jay and the Oneworld team who encouraged me to write – and for Marsha Filion and Kate Smith, who carried the added burden of tactfully and wisely handling my yens: my thanks to them all.

A few philosophical examples and comments in this work derive from my earlier perplexing philosophical puzzles books with Oneworld, now within my *The Big Think Book: Discover Philosophy Through 99 Perplexing Puzzles*. Some more is said in its chapters – and some less.

I also thank Susanne Mathies, Carolyn Price and Thomas Petersen for the translations, sometimes loosely revised by me, of the epigraphs that head the chapters from, respectively, the German (Marx and Nietzsche), classical Greek (Xenophanes and Sophocles, the latter based on R. C. Jebb's 1900 translation) and Danish (Hans Christian Andersen's Polly the parrot). Epigraphs are provocative, as I now discover, in more ways than one. I thank too the Provost and Scholars of King's College, Cambridge, and The Society of Authors as the representatives of E. M. Forster's estate for granting permission to use the two E. M. Forster quotations – and Peter Jones, King's librarian, for his valuable help in this matter.

To avoid roadwork drillings and pointless alarms shrieking, I fled to the British Library; my thanks to the very helpful BL staff, though not – I grumpily add – to those users seemingly unable to work without laptop jingles, mobile phones and frequent sniffs.

For this expanded edition, my thanks to Oneworld's Jonathan Bentley-Smith for helpful ideas and bearing with me; Gerard Livingstone and Martin Holt for philosophical stimulation; Brian Adger for science; John Shand for exposure to his 'glory of freedom' repeated mantra; Kay Walters and Laura Doran of the Athenaeum Library and Laura's wonderfully swift supply of books courtesy of the London Library – and Avril Shorland for good-humoured enhancement of my library labours.

Peter Cave
Soho
London

Appendix 1
Further reading

I owe much to many of the following works and also those listed in Appendix 2's notes. Publication details are usually omitted, when many editions are readily available.

For a steady and clear account, by an active humanist philosopher, see Richard Norman, *On Humanism* (London: Routledge, 2004). A fine collection is Christopher Hitchens, *The Portable Atheist* (Philadelphia: Da Capo, Perseus, 2007). See also Michael Martin, ed., *The Cambridge Companion to Atheism* (Cambridge: CUP, 2007).

Two outstanding classics are David Hume's *Dialogues Concerning Natural Religion* and John Stuart Mill's *Three Essays on Religion*. A 'modern classic' is Bertrand Russell's essay, now introduced by humanist Simon Blackburn, *Why I Am Not a Christian: and Other Essays on Religion and Related Subjects* (London: Routledge, 2004). For existentialism, see Jean-Paul Sartre's *Existentialism and Humanism*, trans. Philip Mairet (London: Methuen, 1948), though Sartre later repudiated parts.

A stimulating read is Christopher Hitchens, *God is Not Great: How Religions Poison Everything* (New York: Twelve, 2007). A lighter work, with a personal anecdotal air, is Richard Dawkins's *The God Delusion* (London: Bantam Press, 2006). It has been much praised and damned. Dawkins is a fine and distinguished chap to have in the humanist camp. He says his book is non-confrontational. Well, if that is non-confrontational …

A. C. Grayling, Simon Blackburn and Daniel Dennett are distinguished humanist philosophers; their writings and talks are well worth engaging. For sustained, humanist-inspired discussions, see A. C. Grayling, *What Is Good?* and *The Choice of Hercules* (London: Weidenfeld and Nicolson, 2002/2007). Other important and accessible philosophers, humanistically inclined, are Jonathan Glover and Peter Singer. Humanity's inhumanity is shown in Jonathan Glover, *Humanity, a Moral History of the Twentieth Century* (London: Jonathan Cape, 1999). For religiously orientated stances, questioning humanism, highly readable philosophers are Roger Scruton and John Cottingham. Returning to humanism itself, see also Jeaneane Fowler, *Humanism: Beliefs and Practices* (Brighton: Sussex Academic Press, 1999).

There are ever-increasing works arguing the case for humanism and, relatedly, secularism. Please see A. C. Grayling and Andrew Copson, eds, *The Wiley Blackwell Handbook of Humanism* (Oxford: Wiley Blackwell, 2015) and for a basic introduction, Alice Roberts, *The Little Book of Humanism: Universal Lessons on Finding Purpose, Meaning, and Joy* (London: Piatkus, 2020). See also works and debates with the humanist case being firmly supported by Arif Ahmed, Andrew Copson, A. C. Grayling, Sam Harris, Stephen Law and Raymond Tallis.

Some puzzles about religion and God are in my *The Big Think Book: Discover Philosophy Through 99 Perplexing Puzzles* (London: Oneworld, 2015) and in co-authored works with Rabbi Dan Cohn-Sherbok, *Jews: Nearly Everything You Wanted To Know – But Were Too Afraid To Ask* (Sheffield: Equinox, 2017) and *Arguing about Judaism: a Rabbi, a Philosopher and a Revealing Debate* (London: Routledge, 2019). More problems about humanist values of liberty, equality and justice are in my *The Myths We Live By: A Contrarian's Guide to Democracy, Free Speech and Other Liberal Fictions* (London: Atlantic Books, 2019).

Many references next are to the internet; it is much required for daily living – yet millions lack access, often through poverty. Humanists promote the inclusive society, seeing such access virtually as important as should be provision of heat and light.

Appendix 2
Notes and references

In order to reduce clutter, sources of many brief quotations are not included, especially when easily found by internet searches. Similarly, publication details are usually omitted, when many editions are readily available. I do, of course, owe lots to many of the works cited. I thank the authors.

Preface to the extended edition

On the internet, there are numerous citations – and arguments – regarding Wikileaks' 2010 exposure of the United States' military and diplomatic activities, mainly concerning Iraq and Afghanistan, as well as the subsequent treatment or mistreatment of Julian Assange. An exploration of the leaks is in Wikileaks, *The Wikileaks Files* (London: Verso, 2016). The video 'Collateral Murder', showing indiscriminate killing by US forces, is available at collateralmurder.wikileaks.org.

For evidence of Saudi Arabia's use of UK-manufactured weapons in Yemen, please see House of Commons briefing paper 08425, *UK arms exports to Saudi Arabia: Q&A*, 29 January 2021, also available online at researchbriefings.files.parliament.uk/documents/ CBP-8425/CBP-8425.pdf, and the government's written evidence for the Committees on Arms Export Controls, from March 2016, available at data.parliament.uk/writtenevidence/ committeeevidence.svc/evidencedocument/committees-on-arms-export-controls/use-of-ukmanufactured-arms-in-yemen/

written/31698.html. Further evidence is cited by the Campaign Against Arms Trade. Many papers from the United Nations set out how the Yemeni Civil War has given rise to the 'largest humanitarian crisis in the world'.

Regarding parliamentary lies by Prime Minister Johnson, please see Peter Oborne, *The Assault on Truth* (London: Simon and Schuster, 2021). Some examples are given by the lawyer Peter Stefanovic at twitter.com/PeterStefanovi2. 'Lie', rather than 'mistake' or 'exaggeration in the heat of the political moment', is used because when errors are pointed out, Johnson refuses to set the record straight. A letter from six MPs to the House of Commons Speaker also lists examples: www.carolinelucas.com/latest/letter-to-the-speaker-about-pms-lies.

The crooked timber quotation is from Kant's 1784 essay 'Idea for a Universal History with a Cosmopolitan Purpose'. Chapter 4 looks at Kant's morality and links to humanism.

Chapter 1, Humanism: scene setting

For 'only connect', see E. M. Forster's 1910 *Howards End*, Chapter 22. The Philip Pullman is from the introduction to *Paradise Lost* (Oxford: OUP, 2005). The Nietzschean extract is from *The Gay Science*, trans. Josefine Nauckhoff (Cambridge: CUP, 2001), though I have used 'greatest' instead of 'heaviest'.

For Renaissance thinkers, see Jill Kraye's *The Cambridge Companion to Renaissance Humanism* (Cambridge: CUP, 1996). A short, detailed survey of 'humanism' labels is Nicolas Walter's *Humanism: What's in the Word* (London: Rationalist Press, 1997). Extracts from famous humanists are in Margaret Knight's *Humanist Anthology*, rev. Jim Herrick (London: Rationalist Press, 1995). A. J. Ayer, ed., *The Humanist Outlook* (London: Pemberton,1968) offers a disparate collection. It includes Sargant Florence's essay, 'The Cambridge Heretics 1909–1932', reminding us of how radical atheism and humanism were considered, even less than a hundred years ago in educated British circles.

'Freddie' Ayer was proud of his humanism. There were worried humanists, when, near his life's end, he wondered whether he underwent some 'out of body' experiences. Ayer remained, though, an empiricist, in the tradition of Hume and Mill. Whether he momentarily weakened or not, he ended as a 'born again atheist'. See Ben Rogers, *A. J. Ayer: A Life* (London: Chatto and Windus, 1999).

John Gray sets humanist hearts racing with indignation with his *Straw Dogs* (London: Granta, 2002); the book is worth a dip, if only to spot exaggerations – mind you, it is not all bad. Information on the many gods, and many more, is at the wonderful www.godchecker.com.

Chapter 2, Without God

A good and thorough examination is Nick Everitt's *The Non-Existence of God* (London: Routledge, 2004). By the way, William Paley's watch in recent decades curiously has been transposed from heath to seashore.

Specifically for evolution, see Richard Dawkins, *The Selfish Gene*, 30th anniversary ed. (Oxford: OUP, 2006). Dawkins likens his book to Ayer's 1936 *Language, Truth and Logic*, a young man's book, full of vigour and highly successful – except, Dawkins adds, that unlike Ayer, he needs to recant nothing of substance. Other geneticists disagree. A reflective approach is Michael Ruse's *Can a Darwinian Be a Christian?* (Cambridge: CUP, 2001).

Anthropic principles are in, for example, Robin Le Poidevin's *Arguing for Atheism* (London: Routledge, 1996). My minimal knowledge of what physicists currently (and probably transiently) claim derives from Martin J. Rees, *Just Six Numbers* (London: Weidenfeld and Nicolson, 1999). Professor Lord Rees of Ludlow, as he now is, is a highly distinguished, humanistic, non-believing Christian; he is Astronomer Royal, Master of Trinity College, Honorary Fellow of King's College, Cambridge, and much more – yet for all that, we should bravely wonder what evidence and sense there is in talk of multiple universes. A discussion of such multiverses is Daniel C. Dennett's 'Atheism and Evolution' in Martin's *Cambridge Companion to Atheism*, cited in 'Further reading'. For some reference to 'condition of possibility', and also an outspoken yet somewhat baffling attack on Dawkins, see Terry Eagleton's 'Lunging, Flailing, Mispunching', *London Review of Books*, 19 October 2006, available online.

Chapter 3, Without religion

I am tempted to mention first the Monty Python film *The Life of Brian* – and I have. It is a fine humanist 'critique' of religion. For more on Marx, see his *A Contribution to the Critique of Hegel's Philosophy of Right: Introduction* (1844) reprinted in *Marx: Early Political Writings*, trans. Joseph O'Malley and Richard A. Davis (Cambridge: CUP, 1994).

Numerous contradictions within the Bible are cited at www.infidels.org. That children are put to death – or not – is at *Deuteronomy* 24.16 and *Isaiah* 41.21. A general discussion of God, faith and religion is Anthony Kenny's *The Unknown God* (London: Continuum, 2004). Kenny left the Catholic priesthood, when a young man, becoming a distinguished Oxford philosopher and agnostic. Another distinguished philosopher, who went the other way, to Catholicism as a young man, is Peter Geach; so, for religious opposition, see his *Providence and Evil* (Cambridge: CUP, 1977). Geach does not mince words.

Despite Plato, some philosophers do ground morality in divine law: try Marilyn McCord Adams and Robert Merrihew Adams, eds, *The Problem of Evil* (Oxford: OUP, 1990). That religion involves stories for moral behaviour is in R. B. Braithwaite's 1955 article 'An Empiricist's View of the Nature of Religion', in Basil Mitchell, ed., *Philosophy of Religion* (Oxford: OUP, 1971). A seminal paper is John Wisdom's 1944 'Gods', in *Philosophy and Psychoanalysis* (Oxford: Blackwell, 1953). For some representations of Christ and the world, see Graham Howes, *The Art of the Sacred* (London: I. B. Tauris, 2007).

Spinoza on God is in his *Ethics.* The curses heaped upon him are in Steven Nadler's *Spinoza's Heresy: Immortality and the Jewish Mind* (Oxford: Clarendon, 2001); and see Spinoza's *Theological-Political Treatise*, ed. Jonathan Israel (Cambridge: CUP, 2007).

Spinoza radically reinterpreted religious language. Matthew Arnold, much later, was influenced by Spinoza, yet also by Cardinal Newman and the Oxford Movement. Arnold struggled with his crisis of faith, at times suggesting 'God' to be a poetic term. Others in the nineteenth century moved to agnosticism, a term coined by T. H. Huxley, who famously defended evolution theory, taking on the Church, in an Oxford debate with Bishop Wilberforce. For non-realist takes on godly talk – amounting to humanism? – see Don Cupitt, *The Sea of Faith*, 2nd ed. (London: SCM, 1994) and Tim Crane, *The Meaning of Belief: Religion from an Atheist's Point of View* (Cambridge M.A.: HUP, 2017).

Chapter 4, With morality

The opening dilemma, from Dostoevsky's *The Karamazov Brothers*, is reprinted in Peter Singer, ed., *Ethics* (Oxford: OUP, 1994), a good collection for much. For moral theories, try Richard Norman, *The Moral Philosophers*, 2nd ed. (Oxford: OUP, 1998).

A key primary source is J. S. Mill's *Utilitarianism*; see also J. J. C. Smart and Bernard Williams, *Utilitarianism: For and Against* (Cambridge: CUP, 1973). Williams's thought-provoking quip 'one thought too many' is in 'Persons, Character and Morality', in *Moral Luck* (Cambridge: CUP, 1981). Bentham's 'natural rights' quotation, commenting on the French Declaration of Rights, is 'natural rights is simple nonsense: natural and imprescriptible rights, rhetorical nonsense, nonsense upon stilts', in *Anarchical Fallacies*, in *Bentham's PoliticalThought*, ed. Bhikhu Parekh (London: Croom Helm, 1973). For this – and the 'pushpin poetry' remark – see Ross Harrison, *Bentham* (London: Routledge, 1983).

Kant's major moral works are *Groundwork of the Metaphysics of Morals* and *The Metaphysics of Morals*, ed. Mary Gregor (Cambridge: CUP, 1998/1996). Roger Scruton's *Kant* (Oxford: OUP, 1982) is an excellent introductory exposition.

Humpty Dumpty's approach is in Lewis Carroll's *Through the Looking Glass*. Emphasis on the case-by-case is in Renford Bambrough's *Moral Scepticism and Moral Knowledge* (London: Routledge, 1979). Bambrough, although little read, deserves reading. The case-by-case approach derives from John Wisdom, cited in Chapter 3's notes, who points out how we adopt this even in logic. Imre Lakatos does likewise in the philosophy of science and F. R. Leavis in literature. I owe the latter observation to Ardon Lyon. The philosopher much read in this area, recognizing ethical muddles, though no philosophical bedfellow of Bambrough, is Bernard Williams: see *Ethics and the Limits of Philosophy* (London: Fontana, 1985).

Chapter 5, With politics

The Forster quotation is from 'What I Believe', in his *Two Cheers for Democracy* (London: Edward Arnold, 1951); also see that for a review of Cavafy. Socrates as gadfly is found in Plato's *Apology*.

A key source for humanist liberalism is J. S. Mill's *On Liberty*. Natural rights, from God, are in John Locke's *Second Treatise of Government*, sometimes seen as a source of libertarianism. 'Liberalism' and 'libertarianism' are somewhat fluid. Locke defended toleration of religious expressions, but, seemingly inconsistently, not of atheism. For more on liberty, liberalism and libertarianism, see Jonathan Wolff's *An Introduction to Political Philosophy* 3rd ed. (Oxford: OUP, 2015).

Regarding difficulties with liberalism and equality – and the thought about lifespans – see John Kekes, *Against Liberalism* and *The Illusions of Egalitarianism* (Ithica, N.Y.: Cornell, 1997/2003). An excellent small book on the public-private is Raymond Geuss's *Public Goods, Private Goods* (Princeton N.J.: Princeton Univ., 2001).

Vast quantities of books, fiction and non-fiction, have been banned because of religious beliefs or doctrines held by atheist states. See Margaret Bald's *Literature Suppressed on Religious Grounds* (New York: Facts on File, 2006). Information on the laws of certain Islamic states, decreeing stoning (the stones must be medium size, to maximize the suffering) and other horrors, is available at the Amnesty International website. It is easy to forget that even in Britain, fifty years ago or so, homosexual activity was still illegal. Alan Turing, the genius of Enigma fame, for example, was in effect hounded to his death because he was openly homosexual. Religious doctrines on sex, in many countries, continue to cause repressed misery for numerous individuals.

Chapter 6, Dying and living

Topics here are well discussed in Jonathan Glover's *Causing Death and Saving Lives* (London: Penguin, 1977) and Peter Singer's *Practical Ethics* 3rd ed. (Cambridge: CUP, 2011). For the emphasis on valuing valuers, see John Harris, *The Value of Life* (London: Routledge, 1985). A version of Mill's pig quip is in his *Utilitarianism*. The sailing tale derives from the Everest example in Robert Nozick's *Anarchy, State, and Utopia* (Oxford: Blackwell, 1974). The Thomson article appears in Peter Singer, ed., *Applied*

Ethics (Oxford: OUP, 1986). For love, try Richard Taylor, *Having Love Affairs* (Buffalo N.Y.: Prometheus, 1982). Sartre's discussion of the student dilemma is in his *Existentialism and Humanism*, cited in 'Further reading'. See Carole Seymour-Jones, *A Dangerous Liaison* (London: Century, 2008), for some rather disreputable aspects of Sartre's life with Simone de Beauvoir. For someone humanistically inclined, concerned about animal rights and the environment, little known yet deserving to be known, try Henry Salt. See George Hendrick and Willene Hendrick, eds, *The Savour of Salt* (Fontwell: Century Press, 1989).

The ethics–morality distinction derives from Bernard Williams: see Chapter 4's notes. Richard Wollheim, sometime London colleague of Williams, comments that we think no less of a painter because he has the odd evening off and gets drunk; so, should we think any less of the moral person having time off from morality? See Wollheim's *The Thread of Life* (Cambridge: CUP, 1984). I owe the reference to Derek Matravers.

Although Williams and Wollheim would have been unhappy with humanist labels, suggesting an organized movement, their attitudes to life were very humanistic. It is appropriate that they were both connected with the godless institution University College London – and that Williams was, for many years, provost of King's College, Cambridge, with its toleration and previous associations with Keynes, Ramsey, Forster, Brooke, Turing, the Bloomsbury Group *et al.* See Williams, *Making Sense of Humanity* (Cambridge: CUP, 1995) and *Philosophy as a Humanistic Discipline*, ed. Adrian Moore (Princeton: Princeton Univ. Press, 2006).

Chapter 7, Humanism: the quest for meaning

An excellent collection is Oswald Hanfling, ed., *Life and Meaning* (Oxford: Blackwell, 1987). Ossie – very atheist and humanist at heart – gave his own take in *The Quest for Meaning* (Oxford: Blackwell, 1987). For a simple 'prisoner's dilemma', see 'Chicken!' in my *The Big Think Book* (London: Oneworld, 2015), where there are further puzzles about life.

Nietzsche's stance is in his 'On Truth and Lies in a Nonmoral Sense', *Philosophy and Truth: Selections from Nietzsche's Notebooks of the Early 1870s*, trans. and ed. Daniel Breazeale (New Jersey: Humanities Press, 1979). Dostoevsky is one who stresses the absurdity of treating people as cogs; see, for example, his *Notes from the Underground*, whence some of my comments derive. The mouse is from Thomas Nagel's *Mortal Questions* (Cambridge: CUP, 1979), where absurdity, death and moral luck are discussed. 'Moral luck' derives from Williams (cited in Chapter 4's notes). The Dawkins' quotation is from *The Selfish Gene* (cited in Chapter 2's notes), p. 332. For a discussion of scientism's errors, try M. R. Bennett and P. M. S. Hacker, *Philosophical Foundations of Neuroscience* (Oxford: Blackwell, 2003).

The McTaggart tale derives from Goldsworthy Lowes Dickinson (1862–1932), a keen humanist. Forster wrote of 'Goldie' that he was neither a great philosopher nor writer nor successful reformer, yet his 'beloved, affectionate, unselfish, intelligent, witty, charming' qualities were fused into him, making him 'a rare being, leaving people who met him more hopeful about other men because he had lived' – an admirable humanist indeed. See E. M. Forster, *Goldsworthy Lowes Dickinson* (London: Edward Arnold, 1934).

G. E. Moore's naturalistic fallacy is in his 1903 *Principia Ethica*, best approached through Thomas Baldwin's revised edition (Cambridge: CUP, 1993). For Moore's humanistic influence on the Bloomsbury Group, see J. M. Keynes's *Two Memoirs* (London: Rupert Hart-Davis, 1949). For F. P. Ramsey, see 'Epilogue' in *Philosophical Papers*, ed. D. H. Mellor (Cambridge: CUP, 1990). Ramsey – Frank Plumpton Ramsey – had a younger brother who, despite recognizing Frank's atheism and greater intelligence, became Archbishop of Canterbury.

The Apollonian and Dionysian are on display in Julian Young, *Nietzsche's Philosophy of Art* (Cambridge: CUP, 1992), to which I am indebted. For some Nietzsche direct on the Apollonian/Dionysian duality, see his *The Birth of Tragedy*. The translation of Nietzsche on nature is by R. J. Hollingdale in Nietzsche, *Beyond Good and Evil* (Harmondsworth: Penguin, 1973). For Mozart, see Julian Rushton, ed., *W. A. Mozart: 'Don Giovanni'* (Cambridge: CUP, 1988). A mesmerizing opera that lifts the spirit, submerges you in sights and sounds, as well as making a humanist political point, with paradoxically Arjuna and Krishna present, is Philip Glass's *Satyagraha*, about M. K. Ghandi – directed by Phelim McDermott for the English National Opera, London, and the Metropolitan Opera, New York (ENO revival, 2021). An outstanding *Salome* production is David McVicar's, Royal Opera House, London (2008).

Chapter 8, Pan-disasters, pan-deceptions and pandemonium

Certain religious leaders have judged the pandemic – and other disasters – as God's displeasure at societies' toleration of the non-religious. God is offended. Hence, in some countries humanists and other free thinkers have been punished. Please see *Freedom of Thought Report* (online), a survey by Humanists International. For separating state from religion, there is Andrew Copson, *Secularism* (Oxford, OUP: 2017).

Regarding pandemic restrictions, the Great Barrington Declaration is online, as is the John Snow Memorandum, a highly critical response. The Declaration's Wikipedia entry provides numerous references supportive, numerous objecting. A good online paper is Stephen Davies, 'COVID-19 and complexity: Hayekian economics and the world after the pandemic'.

For the growth of inequalities in Britain, please see the well-respected and independent reviews by Sir Michael Marmot. In 2018, Philip Alston, then UN special rapporteur, issued a report on UK's extreme poverty and human rights; there, he speaks of the government being 'in denial'. The government's response was to deny it – seemingly blind to the irony in doing.

Hobbes's quotations are from *Leviathan* (1651), available online. As ever, the online *Stanford Encyclopaedia of Philosophy* is reliable and detailed for the philosophical concepts deployed. Vittorio Bufacchi, *Everything Must Change: Philosophical Lessons from Lockdown* (Manchester: MUP, 2021), raises pertinent matters with clarity and compassion.

Turning to climate change, 'Anthropocene' derives from the Greek *anthropo*, 'man', and *cene*, 'new'; it was introduced via Eugene Stoermer and Paul Crutzen. The Intergovernmental Panel on Climate Change has a webpage with the latest scientific thinking on climate change and how best to respond.

Chapter 9, Whither humanism? Whither humanity?

For background, please see Nick Bostrom, 'A History of Transhumanist Thought' (online). Examples of obscure or high-falutin discussions are in Sonia Baelo-Allué and Mónica Calvo-Pascual, eds, *Transhumanism and Posthumanism in Twenty-First Century Narrative* (London: Routledge, 2021). For Nietzsche's relevance (or not), there is Yunus Tuncel, ed., *Nietzsche and Transhumanism: Precursor or Enemy?* (Newcastle: Cambridge Scholars, 2017).

Turning to Rebekah, my *The Myths We Live By: A Contrarian's Guide to Democracy, Free Speech and Other Liberal Fictions* (London: Atlantic, 2019) covers much. See also Sophie Bolat, 'Privacy: its nature, value and protection' (MA Diss., OU, 2012).

Doubts about enhancements are in Michael Sandel, *The Case against Perfection: Ethics in the Age of Genetic Engineering* (Cambridge M.A.: Belknap, 2009). Please see (and hear) TED talks by Nick Bostrom and Julian Savulescu in support of enhancements, available via YouTube.

Regarding other species, Archy provides some splendid thoughts and humour, courtesy of Don Marquis, *The Annotated Archy and Mehitabel* (London: Penguin, 2006). For detailed and careful attention on the importance of animal lives, with a Kantian stance, there is Christine M. Korsgaard, *Fellow Creatures: Our Obligations to the Other Animals* (Oxford: OUP, 2018).

Population dangers are in Thomas Malthus, *An Essay on the Principle of Population* (1798), available online. Challenges to sentient existence as a good are by David Benatar, *Better Never to Have Been: The Harm of Coming into Existence* (New York: OUP, 2006). David Hume's solution for melancholy is in his *An Enquiry Concerning Human Understanding* (1748); he also writes of how he took pleasure in 'the company of modest women' and 'had no reason to be displeased with the reception [he] met with from them' – that is from his short and sweet *My Own Life* (1776), written when he was dying, showing a fine humanist stance towards death.

Expanded discussions on some of these matters are in my *Ethics: A Beginner's Guide*, rev. ed. (London: Oneworld, 2017).

Expanding on speculations of intelligent life going way beyond human beings, some argue, as noted at the end of Chapter 8, that it is highly probable that intelligences, not in biological form, already exist in the universe or 'multiverse'; they may be more akin to what today we understand as instances of 'artificial intelligence', albeit radically advanced. Please see Lord Martin Rees, eminent cosmologist met earlier: for example, his 'Seti: why extraterrestrial intelligence is more likely to be artificial than biological' (2021), available online at: theconversation.com/seti-why-extraterrestrial-intelligence-is-more-likely-to-be-artificial-than-biological-169966. For related puzzles here concerning consciousness, please see the work of Galen Strawson on 'panpsychism'.

Epilogue

The 'I can't go on' mantra is in Samuel Beckett's *The Unnameable* (London: J. Calder, 1959). The mime tale is in Norman Manea's *On Clowns: The Dictator and the Artist* (New York: Grove, 1992). Rupert Brooke, circa 1910, deemed himself Neo-Pagan, though seemed also to be socialist, atheist and intrigued by sex, be it with man or woman. 'A slight angle to the universe' is a reference to E. M. Forster's description of C. P. Cavafy. See C. P. Cavafy, *The Collected Poems* (Oxford: OUP, 2007).

For more reflections on humanity, the humanities and what it is to be human, please see the works of Raymond Geuss, for example, *Who Needs a World View?* (Cambridge M.A.: Harvard Univ. Press, 2020); Stefan Collini, *Speaking of Universities* (London: Verso, 2017); and Raymond Tallis, *Seeing Ourselves* (Newcastle upon Tyne: Agenda, 2020).

Humanists need not be blind to *Spem in alium*'s beauty. Many of us – happy to give metaphorical interpretations – are untroubled by its words: 'I have never founded my hope upon other than thee, O God of Israel, who shall be angry and yet gracious ...'

And so – and so – I end this extended edition, as I began the original work: an atheist, humanist and convinced that there is no afterlife. I can, though, still find value and meaning within life – even, indeed, a touch of eternity. As I have written elsewhere (in *The Big Think Book*):

All the things we value, however rare, however small, that give point or meaning within our lives – the friendships, loves, humours and absurdities; those soundscaped memories entwined with shared passions and glances that magically ensnare and enfold; the intoxications of wines and words, of music and wonder and wayward musings, with which we wrestle into misty slumbering nights, our senses revived by sparkling waters, much needed at dawn; the seascapes of wild waves, mysterious moonlights and images and widening skies that stretch the eyes – do indeed all cease to exist; and curiously the most enchanting are often those within which we lose ourselves and also cease to be – yet that they, and we, existed at some time remains timelessly true, outside of all time.

For lovers of eternity, that is as good as it gets. And is not that good enough?

Blow, bugle, blow, set the wild echoes flying,
And answer, echoes, answer, dying, dying, dying.

Tennyson

Index

References to entire chapters are in **bold**.

More philosophy from Peter Cave in Oneworld's Beginner's Guides

'I wish this book had been my introduction to philosophy.'
William Irwin, Professor of Philosophy, King's College Pennsylvania

Philosophy, the 'love of wisdom', is the product of our endless fascination and curiosity about the world. Through it, we seek to answer the most fundamental of questions: How do we know what we know? Does God exist? What am I?

Peter Cave navigates all the main topics with verve and clarity in this exhilarating tour.

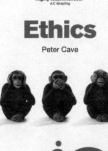

'An excellent primer. Highly recommended!'
A. C. Grayling

Why is it important to act morally?

With his characteristic wit, Peter Cave steers us around well-known and not-so-well-known ethical traps – in the private and public spheres, and in relation to God and religion – in this introduction to the most popular branch of philosophy.